INSPIRING BASKETBALL
LEGENDS STORIES FOR TEENS

Trivia Book

Motivational Basketball GOATS Stories, Incredible Facts, and Trivia Games! (Young Readers' Sports Books)

CONTENT

Introduction

Part 1: The Rise Of Basketball Legends

    Chapter 1: Introduction To Basketball

    Chapter 2: From Gymnasiums To Global Arenas

    Chapter 3: The 20th-Century Boom

    Chapter 4: The Nba's International Influence

    Chapter 5: Basketball's Cultural Impact

Part 2: The Legends Of Basketball

    Chapter 1: Basketball's Early Heroes

    Chapter 2: Golden Era Superstars

    Chapter 3: Modern-Day Icons

    Chapter 4: The Record Breakers And Trailblazers

Part 3: Interactive Games & Challenges

    Chapter 1: True-False Section

Chapter 2: Player And Court Questions

Chapter 3: Advanced Trivia Challenges

Chapter 4: Notebook Pages

INTRODUCTION

Get ready to dive into the exciting world of basketball with **"Inspiring Basketball Legends Stories for Teens"** – a book packed with motivational tales of legendary players, fun facts, and interactive trivia games that will captivate every young sports fan! This book is perfect for teens who love basketball or those just discovering the magic of the game, offering engaging stories that celebrate the greatest players of all time – from Michael Jordan and LeBron James to Caitlin Clark!

What Makes This Book Special:

- **Legendary Stories of Basketball GOATs :** Explore the journeys of the best players in basketball history, with stories that inspire and showcase how hard work, perseverance, and a love for the game can lead to greatness.
- **Interactive Trivia & Games :** Test your knowledge with fun trivia questions and challenges that make reading interactive and entertaining, similar to the fun of Alexa interactive books for kids.
- **Incredible Basketball Facts :** Just like the fascinating details in the Sports Almanac from Back to the Future, this book is loaded with stats, records, and cool facts about basketball legends that will amaze any sports enthusiast.
- **Inspirational Role Models :** Following the motivational tone of books like the Average Boy Books, this book encourages teens to set goals, stay focused, and be inspired by real-life role models in the world of sports.

Why Teens Will Love It:

This book isn't just about basketball – it's about life lessons. Each story reveals how these players overcame obstacles, dedicated themselves to the game, and made history. It's perfect for readers who enjoy the engaging narratives of The Magic School Bus Inside the Human Body or the excitement of solving mysteries in the Detective Duck Books Series. This book keeps young readers hooked from page to page with fascinating facts and interactive content.

Perfect Gift for Young Basketball Fans :

Looking for a gift for a teen who loves basketball? This book is a fantastic choice! Not only does it cover famous players, but it also includes rising stars like Caitlin Clark – a player who is making waves in the game, perfect for young fans to relate to. Think of it as a Caitlin Clark book for kids, designed to inspire and motivate the next generation.

Whether you're on the sidelines cheering, watching your favorite team on TV, or dreaming of your own place on the court, **"Inspiring Basketball Legends Stories for Teens"** is a must-read! This book combines the excitement of basketball with interactive fun, making it more than just a book – it's a journey into the heart of the game.

PART 1:

THE RISE OF BASKETBALL LEGENDS

Chapter 1:
INTRODUCTION TO BASKETBALL

In the winter of 1891, Dr. James Naismith, a Canadian physical education instructor at Springfield College in Massachusetts, was tasked with creating a new indoor game for his students. The goal was to develop an activity that would keep the young men active and engaged during the cold winter months, bridging the gap between football and baseball seasons. Naismith sought a game that was less prone to injuries than these popular sports, emphasizing skill and finesse over brute strength.

His solution was basketball, a game initially played with two peach baskets nailed to the lower railing of the gymnasium balcony, and a soccer ball. The objective was simple: throw the ball into the opposing team's basket. Naismith devised thirteen original rules, which included elements like no running with the ball, no tackling, and the use of both hands to handle the ball. These rules aimed to promote teamwork and minimize physical contact, making the game safe and engaging for all players.

The first game was played in December 1891 with nine players on each team. The court was half the size of a regulation court today, and players used a soccer ball. Interestingly, the bottom of the peach baskets was intact, meaning that after each successful shot, the ball had to be retrieved manually using a ladder. It wasn't until a few years later that the bottoms of the baskets were removed, allowing for continuous play.

Basketball was a unique creation for its time. Unlike other popular sports, it was designed specifically for indoor play and emphasized passing and shooting accuracy over physical dominance. The game quickly gained popularity among students at Springfield College and soon spread to other schools and YMCAs across the country.

From its humble beginnings as a school activity, basketball has evolved into a global phenomenon, captivating audiences worldwide with its fast-paced action, intricate strategies, and remarkable athleticism. Yet, the core principles of teamwork, skill, and sportsmanship instilled by Dr. Naismith remain at the heart of the game.

The early years of basketball were marked by rapid evolution and adaptation. As the game spread to different schools and communities, variations in rules and gameplay emerged. Some played with closed-bottom baskets, while others adopted open ones. The number of players on the court fluctuated, and the size of the ball varied. Despite these inconsistencies, the core elements of Naismith's game – teamwork, shooting, and dribbling – remained central.

A significant turning point in basketball's history came with the formation of the National Basketball Association (NBA) in 1946. The NBA standardized the rules and provided a platform for the best players in the world to showcase their skills. Legends like George Mikan, Bill Russell, and Wilt Chamberlain emerged, captivating audiences with their athleticism and dominance. The league's popularity soared, and basketball's reach extended far beyond the borders of the United States.

The game continued to evolve throughout the 20th century. The introduction of the 24-second shot clock in 1954 injected a new level of excitement and strategy, forcing teams to play at a faster pace. The three-point line, adopted by the NBA in 1979, revolutionized offensive strategies and gave rise to a new breed of sharpshooting players.

Today, basketball is a truly global sport, played and enjoyed by millions around the world. From the NBA to international competitions like the Olympics and the FIBA World Cup, the game continues to evolve, with new stars and innovations emerging all the time. And while the high-flying dunks and dazzling ball-handling skills of modern players may seem a far cry from the peach baskets and soccer ball of Naismith's original game, the essence of basketball remains the same: a game of skill, teamwork, and sportsmanship, enjoyed by people of all ages and backgrounds.

Beyond the professional courts, basketball has also become a powerful force for social change. In the United States, the game played a crucial role in breaking down racial barriers, with African American players like Earl Lloyd, Chuck Cooper, and Nat "Sweetwater" Clifton paving the way for future generations. Basketball provided opportunities for athletes from marginalized communities to showcase their talents and achieve success, challenging stereotypes and inspiring social progress.

Moreover, basketball has become a universal language, transcending cultural and linguistic differences. From the bustling street courts of New York City to the remote villages of Africa and Asia, the game fosters connections and builds communities. Its simplicity and accessibility make it a popular sport for people of all ages and abilities, promoting physical fitness, teamwork, and social interaction.

Looking to the future, basketball's global impact is only set to grow. The rise of social media and digital platforms has expanded the game's reach, connecting fans and players from all corners of the globe. New technologies are being integrated into the sport, from advanced analytics that track player performance to virtual reality experiences that immerse fans in the action.

As basketball continues to evolve, it carries with it the legacy of Dr. James Naismith, a visionary educator who sought to create a game that would benefit his students both physically and mentally. His creation has far surpassed his initial expectations, becoming a global phenomenon that continues to inspire and entertain millions around the world. The story of basketball is a testament to the power of human ingenuity and the enduring appeal of a game that celebrates skill, teamwork, and the pursuit of excellence.

The future of basketball holds exciting possibilities. The rise of women's basketball is challenging traditional gender roles and inspiring a new generation of athletes. Leagues like the WNBA are gaining increasing popularity and recognition, showcasing the incredible skill and athleticism of female players. The continued growth of women's basketball promises to further diversify the sport and expand its global impact.

Furthermore, technological advancements are shaping the future of the game. Virtual reality and augmented reality are creating immersive experiences for fans, allowing them to feel like they are courtside or even participating in the action. Advanced analytics are providing coaches and players with unprecedented insights into game strategy and player performance, leading to new levels of optimization and competition.

Basketball's global reach is also expanding into new frontiers. The game is gaining popularity in countries where it was once a niche sport, with grassroots programs and international competitions fostering its growth. This expansion is bringing new talent and perspectives to the game, enriching its diversity and global appeal.

However, the future of basketball also presents challenges. Issues such as player safety, competitive balance, and the influence of money in the sport require careful consideration and proactive solutions. The basketball community must work together to ensure that the game remains fair, accessible, and sustainable for future generations.

Despite these challenges, the future of basketball is bright. The game's enduring appeal lies in its simplicity, its dynamism, and its ability to bring people together. From the schoolyards to the professional arenas, basketball continues to inspire, entertain, and unite people across cultures and continents. As the game continues to evolve, it carries with it the legacy of Dr. James Naismith, a reminder that a simple game can have a profound impact on the world.

Chapter 2:
FROM GYMNASIUMS TO GLOBAL ARENAS

Basketball's journey from a humble gym class activity to a global phenomenon is a fascinating tale of innovation, perseverance, and cultural impact. Here's how that journey unfolded:

Early Growth and the Rise of Organized Leagues:

- From YMCA to Colleges: After its invention in 1891, basketball quickly spread through YMCAs across the United States, becoming a popular recreational activity. Its adoption by colleges in the early 1900s was crucial, leading to the development of standardized rules and organized competitions.
- The Birth of Professional Leagues: The first professional leagues emerged in the early 20th century, but these were often short-lived and lacked stability. The formation of the National Basketball League (NBL) in 1937 marked a significant step towards a more organized and professional structure.
- The NBA Takes Center Stage: In 1946, the Basketball Association of America (BAA) was founded, and three years later, it merged with the NBL to form the National Basketball Association (NBA). This marked a turning point, establishing a dominant league that would become synonymous with professional basketball.

Key Events and Turning Points:

- Television and Media Exposure: The advent of televised games in the 1950s and 60s brought basketball into the homes of millions, dramatically

increasing its visibility and popularity. Iconic moments like Bill Russell's dominance with the Boston Celtics and Wilt Chamberlain's 100-point game captivated audiences and fueled the sport's growth.
- The Rise of International Basketball: While the NBA flourished in the US, the International Basketball Federation (FIBA), founded in 1932, fostered the growth of basketball worldwide. International competitions like the Olympics and the FIBA World Cup showcased the global appeal of the game and introduced international stars to a wider audience.
- Sponsorships and Marketing: As basketball's popularity soared, major brands recognized its marketing potential. Sponsorships and endorsements deals brought significant financial investment into the sport, further fueling its growth and professionalization.
- The Michael Jordan Era: The arrival of Michael Jordan in the 1980s propelled basketball to new heights. His extraordinary talent, charisma, and global appeal transcended the sport, making him a cultural icon and attracting a new generation of fans worldwide.
- The Dream Team and Global Expansion: The 1992 US Olympic "Dream Team," featuring Jordan and other NBA superstars, dominated the competition and captured the world's imagination. This further cemented basketball's status as a global sport and inspired aspiring players around the globe.

The NBA and FIBA's Role:

- The NBA's Global Outreach: The NBA has actively promoted basketball internationally through exhibition games, player development programs, and partnerships with foreign leagues. This has expanded the league's fanbase and created opportunities for international players to compete at the highest level.
- FIBA's Development Programs: FIBA has played a crucial role in developing basketball infrastructure and talent worldwide. Through youth programs, coaching

clinics, and international competitions, FIBA has fostered the growth of the game in countries across the globe.

Basketball's transformation from a school sport to a global phenomenon is a testament to its adaptability, its exciting nature, and its ability to connect people across cultures. The NBA and FIBA have played pivotal roles in this journey, and the future of basketball promises even greater global reach and impact.

As basketball continues its global ascent, several trends are shaping its future and ensuring its continued relevance in an ever-changing world:

- The Rise of Social Media: Social media platforms have become essential tools for connecting fans, players, and teams. They provide unprecedented access to behind-the-scenes content, player interactions, and real-time game updates, fostering a sense of community and engagement among fans worldwide. This also allows players to build their own brands and connect directly with fans, further blurring the lines between the personal and the professional.
- Basketball and Social Justice: Increasingly, players and leagues are using their platforms to advocate for social justice and address important societal issues. This activism is raising awareness, sparking conversations, and inspiring change, demonstrating the power of basketball to transcend the court and contribute to a better world.
- E-sports and Gaming: The rise of e-sports has opened up new avenues for basketball fans to engage with the game. Competitive video game tournaments featuring basketball simulations like NBA 2K are attracting large audiences and blurring the lines between traditional sports and digital entertainment.
- Globalization of the Game: The NBA and FIBA are actively investing in developing basketball talent and

infrastructure in new markets. This is leading to a more diverse pool of players at the highest level and expanding the game's reach into new territories. Leagues in Asia, Africa, and South America are growing in popularity, further contributing to the globalization of the sport.
- Emphasis on Player Development: With a focus on long-term athlete health and performance, leagues and organizations are investing in comprehensive player development programs. These programs emphasize skill development, injury prevention, and mental health, ensuring the well-being of athletes and the sustainability of the sport.

Basketball's journey from a simple gym game to a global phenomenon is a testament to its enduring appeal and its ability to adapt to changing times. With its rich history, its passionate fanbase, and its ongoing evolution, basketball is poised to continue captivating audiences and inspiring generations to come. As the game continues to grow and evolve, it will undoubtedly leave its mark on the world, both on and off the court.

The story of basketball's future is not just about expanding its reach, but also about deepening its impact:

- Focus on Sustainability: As the sport grows, so does its responsibility towards the environment. Leagues and organizations are increasingly adopting sustainable practices, from reducing waste and energy consumption in arenas to promoting eco-friendly merchandise and transportation.
- Basketball as a Tool for Development: Recognizing its power to engage and inspire young people, basketball is being used as a tool for social and economic development in underserved communities around the world. Programs that combine basketball training with educational opportunities and life skills development are empowering youth and fostering positive change.

- Innovation in Training and Performance: Technology continues to revolutionize how players train and prepare for competition. Virtual reality simulations, wearable sensors, and advanced analytics are providing personalized insights and optimizing performance, pushing the boundaries of athletic potential.
- The Evolution of Fan Engagement: The way fans experience basketball is constantly evolving. From interactive mobile apps and virtual reality experiences to personalized content and behind-the-scenes access, technology is creating new ways for fans to connect with the game and their favorite players.
- The Power of Storytelling: Basketball's impact extends beyond the court, with its stories of triumph, perseverance, and teamwork resonating with audiences worldwide. Documentaries, films, and other media are capturing these stories, inspiring and entertaining while showcasing the human side of the sport.

Ultimately, the future of basketball is about more than just the game itself. It's about leveraging the sport's global platform to promote positive values, inspire social change, and connect people across cultures. As basketball continues to evolve, it carries with it the potential to make a meaningful difference in the world, one basket at a time.

Chapter 3:
THE 20TH-CENTURY BOOM

The 20th century witnessed the remarkable transformation of basketball from a fledgling sport invented in a Springfield, Massachusetts gymnasium into a global phenomenon captivating millions worldwide. Here's a look at the key events and figures that fueled this incredible journey:

Early Growth and Collegiate Dominance (1900s-1940s):

- The Rise of College Basketball: Basketball quickly gained popularity in colleges across the United States, with fierce rivalries and legendary players emerging. The NCAA tournament, first held in 1939, became a major sporting event, showcasing the talent and excitement of college basketball.
- The Original Celtics: This barnstorming team, formed in 1914, dominated the early professional scene, showcasing a fast-paced and skillful style of play that helped popularize the sport.
- The Harlem Globetrotters: Founded in 1926, the Globetrotters captivated audiences with their unique blend of athleticism, showmanship, and comedic routines, introducing basketball to new audiences and breaking down racial barriers.

The Birth of the NBA and Professionalization (1940s-1960s):

- Formation of the NBA: The merger of the National Basketball League (NBL) and the Basketball Association of America (BAA) in 1949 created the National Basketball Association (NBA), providing a

stable and organized platform for professional basketball to flourish.
- Early NBA Stars: Legends like George Mikan, the league's first dominant big man, and Bob Cousy, a dazzling ball-handler, captivated fans and helped establish the NBA as a major sports league.
- The Celtics Dynasty: Led by Bill Russell, an unparalleled defensive force, the Boston Celtics dominated the NBA in the 1950s and 60s, winning 11 championships in 13 years and establishing a legacy of excellence.

Global Expansion and Media Influence (1960s-1980s):

- The Rise of International Basketball: The FIBA World Cup and the Olympic Games showcased the global appeal of basketball, with international stars like Sergei Belov (Soviet Union) and Dražen Petrović (Yugoslavia) captivating audiences worldwide.
- Television and Media Coverage: Increased television coverage brought basketball into homes around the world, exposing the sport to new audiences and creating iconic moments that captured the public imagination.
- The ABA and its Impact: The American Basketball Association (ABA), a rival league to the NBA, introduced exciting innovations like the three-point line and a more flamboyant style of play, further fueling basketball's popularity.

The Modern Era and Global Superstardom (1980s-2000s):

- The Magic Johnson vs. Larry Bird Rivalry: This epic rivalry between the Los Angeles Lakers and the Boston Celtics captivated fans throughout the 1980s, showcasing contrasting styles and personalities that defined a generation of basketball.
- The Michael Jordan Era: Michael Jordan's arrival in the NBA ushered in a new era of athleticism, marketing, and global superstardom. His dominance on the court

and his cultural impact off the court propelled basketball to unprecedented heights.
- The Dream Team and Olympic Glory: The 1992 US Olympic "Dream Team," featuring Jordan, Magic Johnson, Larry Bird, and other NBA superstars, dominated the competition and captured the world's imagination, further solidifying basketball's global appeal.

The 21st Century and Beyond:

- International Expansion: The NBA continued its global outreach, with international players becoming increasingly prominent in the league and the game spreading to new markets around the world.
- The Rise of Social Media: Social media platforms provided new avenues for fan engagement and player interaction, further connecting basketball with a global audience.

The growth of basketball in the 20th century is a testament to its exciting nature, its adaptability, and its ability to transcend cultural boundaries. Through the efforts of visionary leaders, talented athletes, and advancements in media, basketball has become a truly global sport, inspiring millions and leaving an indelible mark on the world of sports.

As we move deeper into the 21st century, basketball continues to evolve at a rapid pace, driven by forces both on and off the court:

The Rise of Women's Basketball:

- WNBA's Growing Prominence: The Women's National Basketball Association (WNBA), founded in 1996, has steadily gained recognition and popularity, showcasing the incredible athleticism and skill of female players. Stars like Sue Bird, Diana Taurasi, and Breanna Stewart have become household names, inspiring

young girls and challenging traditional gender roles in sports.
- Increased Media Coverage: Increased media coverage of women's basketball is bringing greater visibility to the league and its players, fostering a growing fanbase and creating new opportunities for female athletes.

Technological Advancements:

- Advanced Analytics: The use of data analysis and statistics is transforming how teams scout players, develop strategies, and evaluate performance. This data-driven approach is leading to new levels of efficiency and competition.
- Virtual Reality and Immersive Experiences: Virtual reality technology is creating new ways for fans to experience the game, offering immersive perspectives and behind-the-scenes access.
- Wearable Technology: Wearable sensors are providing real-time data on player performance, helping to optimize training, prevent injuries, and improve on-court decision-making.

Social and Cultural Impact:

- Basketball as a Platform for Social Change: Players are increasingly using their platforms to advocate for social justice, raise awareness about important issues, and inspire positive change in their communities.
- Globalization and Cultural Exchange: Basketball continues to serve as a bridge between cultures, bringing people together from different backgrounds and promoting understanding and respect.
- Inspiring the Next Generation: Basketball's stories of perseverance, teamwork, and achievement continue to inspire young people around the world, fostering dreams and promoting positive values.

The future of basketball is filled with exciting possibilities. As the sport continues to evolve, it will undoubtedly maintain its position as a global phenomenon, captivating audiences, fostering communities, and inspiring generations to come. The journey that began in a small gymnasium in Massachusetts has led to a global stage where the game continues to grow, innovate, and leave its mark on the world.

The narrative of basketball's future is not just one of expansion and technological advancement, but also of introspection and social responsibility:

Addressing Challenges:

- Competitive Balance: As the NBA becomes increasingly global, maintaining competitive balance between teams with varying resources and access to talent becomes crucial. Innovative solutions like salary cap adjustments and draft reforms might be necessary to ensure fairness and sustained excitement.
- Player Safety: With the increasing athleticism and intensity of the game, player safety is paramount. The league is constantly researching and implementing new rules and technologies to minimize the risk of injuries and protect the long-term health of athletes.
- Mental Health Awareness: The pressures and demands of professional sports can take a toll on athletes' mental health. Leagues and organizations are increasingly prioritizing mental health resources and support systems to ensure the well-being of players.

Expanding the Basketball Ecosystem:

- Youth Development and Grassroots Programs: Investing in youth development programs and grassroots initiatives is essential for ensuring the future of the sport. These programs not only cultivate talent but also promote healthy lifestyles and positive values among young people.
- Basketball for All: Making basketball accessible to people of all ages, abilities, and backgrounds is crucial for fostering inclusivity and promoting the sport's

positive impact. This includes initiatives to support adaptive sports programs and create opportunities for underserved communities.
- Basketball and Education: Integrating basketball with educational programs can create powerful opportunities for personal and academic growth. Scholarships, mentorship programs, and initiatives that promote life skills development through basketball can empower young people and open doors to a brighter future.

Basketball as a Force for Good:

- Environmental Sustainability: As a global sport with a massive following, basketball has a responsibility to minimize its environmental impact. Leagues and organizations are increasingly adopting sustainable practices and promoting environmental awareness.
- Social Justice and Equality: Basketball has a long history of breaking down barriers and promoting social justice. The sport continues to be a platform for athletes and organizations to advocate for equality, raise awareness about important issues, and inspire positive change.
- Global Citizenship and Community Building: Basketball's global reach provides unique opportunities to foster cross-cultural understanding and build strong communities. By promoting values of teamwork, respect, and fair play, basketball can contribute to a more connected and harmonious world.

The future of basketball is a story that is still being written. It's a story of innovation, social responsibility, and the enduring power of sport to inspire, unite, and create positive change. As the game continues to evolve, it will undoubtedly leave its mark on the world, both on and off the court, for generations to come.

Chapter 4:
THE NBA'S INTERNATIONAL INFLUENCE

The NBA's impact on basketball's global growth is undeniable. It's more than just a league; it's a cultural ambassador, actively promoting the sport and engaging fans worldwide. Here's how they've done it:

1. International Games:

- Preseason and Regular Season Games Abroad: The NBA has been playing preseason games outside the US since 1978, but in 2011, they started holding regular-season games abroad as well. This brings the authentic NBA experience to international fans, showcasing the league's best talent and building excitement.
- Global Games: These games have been held in countries like Mexico, Japan, China, England, and France, exposing millions to the NBA product firsthand.

2. Partnerships and Initiatives:

- Basketball Without Borders: This global basketball development and community outreach program brings together young players from different countries to learn from NBA players and coaches. It promotes friendship, healthy living, and education through basketball.
- NBA Academies: These elite training centers around the world identify and develop top young players

outside the US, providing them with resources and opportunities to reach their potential.
- Partnerships with Local Leagues: The NBA collaborates with leagues in other countries, sharing expertise and resources to help develop basketball infrastructure and talent globally.

3. Media Distribution and Digital Presence:

- Global Broadcast Partnerships: NBA games are televised in over 200 countries and territories in 50 languages. This ensures that fans worldwide can follow their favorite teams and players.
- NBA League Pass: This subscription service allows fans to watch live and on-demand games, further expanding access to the NBA.
- Social Media Engagement: The NBA has a massive social media presence, connecting with fans worldwide through platforms like Facebook, Twitter, and Instagram. They create localized content and engage with fans in different languages, fostering a global community.

Impact and Reach:

- Growing International Fanbase: A 2020 Nielsen study found that the NBA has over 1 billion fans worldwide, with significant growth in markets like China, India, and Africa.
- International Players in the NBA: The NBA has become increasingly diverse, with players from over 40 countries represented in the league. This international talent adds to the excitement and global appeal of the game.
- Economic Impact: The NBA's global presence generates significant economic activity through merchandise sales, sponsorships, and tourism.

Anecdotes:

- Yao Ming's Impact on China: Yao Ming's NBA career sparked a basketball boom in China, with millions tuning in to watch him play. This led to increased interest in the NBA and the growth of basketball in the country.
- The Toronto Raptors' Championship: The Toronto Raptors' 2019 NBA championship, led by a diverse roster with players from Cameroon, Spain, and the US, demonstrated the global appeal of the NBA and inspired fans worldwide.

The NBA's strategic efforts have been instrumental in making basketball a truly global sport. By bringing the game to international audiences, investing in youth development, and leveraging media and technology, the NBA has created a global community of basketball fans and solidified its position as a leader in international sports.

The NBA's journey to becoming a global force is far from over. The league continues to push boundaries and explore new frontiers, ensuring that basketball's reach extends to every corner of the world:

Emerging Markets and Future Growth:

- Africa: The NBA is making significant investments in Africa, with initiatives like the Basketball Africa League (BAL) showcasing the continent's burgeoning talent and fostering basketball development. This league, a partnership between the NBA and FIBA, is cultivating a new generation of African players and fans, contributing to the sport's growth and popularity across the continent.
- India: With a massive population and a growing interest in basketball, India represents a significant opportunity for the NBA. The league is actively engaging with fans through grassroots programs, digital content, and partnerships with local organizations, aiming to cultivate a strong basketball culture in the country.

- Latin America: Building on the existing popularity of basketball in countries like Mexico and Argentina, the NBA is expanding its presence in Latin America. This includes hosting games, developing talent through academies, and creating localized content to engage with the region's passionate fanbase.

Innovation and the Future of Fan Engagement:

- Next-Gen Technology: The NBA is embracing cutting-edge technologies to enhance the fan experience. This includes exploring augmented reality (AR) and virtual reality (VR) applications to create immersive viewing experiences, personalized content delivery, and interactive fan engagement opportunities.
- Esports and Gaming: The NBA 2K League, a professional esports league featuring the popular basketball video game, is attracting a new generation of fans and blurring the lines between traditional sports and digital entertainment. This platform provides new avenues for fan engagement and global competition.
- Direct-to-Consumer Content: The NBA is exploring new ways to deliver content directly to fans, bypassing traditional media channels. This could include exclusive behind-the-scenes access, personalized content streams, and interactive experiences that deepen fan engagement.

Social Responsibility and Global Impact:

- Promoting Health and Wellness: The NBA is leveraging its platform to promote healthy lifestyles and encourage physical activity among young people worldwide. Through programs like Jr. NBA, the league is teaching fundamental skills and promoting the values of teamwork, sportsmanship, and leadership.
- Empowering Communities: The NBA is committed to using its influence to address social issues and empower communities around the world. This includes

initiatives to promote education, combat poverty, and advocate for social justice.
- Building Bridges Through Sport: Basketball's universal appeal transcends cultural and linguistic barriers, making it a powerful tool for fostering understanding and building bridges between people worldwide. The NBA is committed to using the sport to promote peace, unity, and global citizenship.

The NBA's vision for the future extends beyond the court, encompassing a global community of fans, players, and partners united by a shared passion for basketball. By embracing innovation, promoting social responsibility, and continuing its global outreach, the NBA is ensuring that basketball's impact will be felt for generations to come.

The NBA's evolution into a global powerhouse is a testament to its adaptability and forward-thinking approach. As the world changes, so too does the league, constantly innovating and finding new ways to connect with fans and grow the game:

Embracing the Digital Age:

- Personalized Content: The NBA is increasingly using data and analytics to understand fan preferences and deliver personalized content. This could involve customized game highlights, player-specific news feeds, and interactive experiences tailored to individual interests.
- Augmented Reality (AR) Integration: Imagine watching a game and seeing real-time player stats overlaid on the screen through your phone or AR glasses, or even having virtual players appear in your living room for a personalized training session. The NBA is exploring these possibilities to create immersive and engaging fan experiences.
- The Metaverse and Web3: The NBA is exploring opportunities in the metaverse, creating virtual spaces where fans can interact with each other, attend virtual

games, and purchase digital collectibles. This could open up new avenues for fan engagement and revenue generation.

Building a Sustainable Future:

- Environmental Initiatives: The NBA is committed to reducing its environmental footprint through initiatives like energy-efficient arenas, sustainable merchandise, and carbon offset programs. They are also using their platform to promote environmental awareness and encourage fans to adopt sustainable practices.
- Social Impact Investing: The NBA is increasingly investing in social impact initiatives that address issues like poverty, inequality, and climate change. This includes supporting organizations that promote education, health, and economic development in underserved communities around the world.

Cultivating the Next Generation of Talent:

- Global Scouting and Development: The NBA is expanding its scouting network and development programs to identify and nurture talent in every corner of the globe. This includes investing in grassroots programs, academies, and international competitions to provide opportunities for young players to reach their full potential.
- Women's Basketball Development: The WNBA continues to grow in popularity and influence, and the NBA is committed to supporting its development and promoting gender equality in basketball. This includes investing in grassroots programs, expanding media coverage, and creating opportunities for female athletes to thrive.

Basketball as a Unifying Force:

- Cultural Diplomacy: The NBA's global reach makes it a powerful platform for cultural exchange and diplomacy. By bringing people together from different backgrounds

and promoting values of teamwork, respect, and sportsmanship, the NBA can foster understanding and build bridges between nations.
- Celebrating Diversity: The NBA is a melting pot of cultures, with players and fans from all over the world. The league celebrates this diversity and uses its platform to promote inclusivity and combat discrimination.

The NBA's journey is a testament to the power of sports to transcend borders and connect people. By embracing innovation, promoting social responsibility, and continuing to grow the game globally, the NBA is shaping the future of basketball and leaving a lasting legacy on the world.

Chapter 5:
BASKETBALL'S CULTURAL IMPACT

Basketball's cultural significance extends far beyond the hardwood, permeating music, fashion, entertainment, and even language. It's more than just a sport; it's a global cultural phenomenon that has shaped and been shaped by popular culture.

Global Fanbase and Reach:

- Over 1 Billion Fans: According to a Nielsen study, the NBA alone boasts a fanbase exceeding 1 billion people worldwide. This massive following translates to a powerful cultural influence, particularly among younger generations.
- Social Media Dominance: Basketball players are among the most followed athletes on social media, with millions of fans engaging with their content daily. This constant interaction reinforces basketball's presence in popular culture and creates a direct connection between athletes and fans.

Basketball and Music:

- Hip-Hop Culture: Basketball and hip-hop have a symbiotic relationship, with countless songs referencing the sport, its players, and its culture. Artists like Jay-Z, Drake, and Kendrick Lamar frequently incorporate basketball themes into their music, further solidifying the sport's place in popular culture.
- Soundtracks and Anthems: From classic films like "Space Jam" to the official NBA theme song, basketball

has inspired memorable soundtracks and anthems that have become part of the cultural lexicon.

Basketball and Fashion:

- Sneaker Culture: Basketball sneakers have transcended their athletic purpose to become fashion staples. Iconic shoes like Air Jordans and Converse Chuck Taylors are worn by people of all ages and backgrounds, reflecting basketball's influence on style and self-expression.
- Athletes as Fashion Icons: Basketball players are often trendsetters, influencing fashion trends with their on- and off-court style. Collaborations between athletes and fashion brands further blur the lines between sports and fashion.

Basketball and Entertainment:

- Movies and Television: Basketball has been featured prominently in films like "Hoosiers," "White Men Can't Jump," and "Coach Carter," showcasing the drama, excitement, and cultural significance of the sport.
- Video Games: Basketball video games like NBA 2K have become incredibly popular, allowing fans to immerse themselves in the sport and connect with their favorite players and teams.

Iconic Rivalries and Teams:

- Lakers vs. Celtics: This historic rivalry, spanning decades, has produced some of the most memorable moments in NBA history. The battles between Magic Johnson and Larry Bird in the 1980s, and later between Kobe Bryant and Paul Pierce, captivated audiences and contributed to the sport's cultural mystique.
- The Chicago Bulls Dynasty: The Chicago Bulls' dominance in the 1990s, led by Michael Jordan, transcended sports and became a global cultural phenomenon. The team's success, combined with

Jordan's iconic status, cemented basketball's place in popular culture.

Basketball's Cultural Impact:

- Global Language: Basketball has become a universal language, uniting people from different backgrounds and cultures through a shared passion for the sport.
- Symbol of Achievement: Basketball represents aspiration and achievement, with players serving as role models for young people around the world.
- Source of Community and Identity: Basketball fosters a sense of community and belonging, bringing people together to celebrate the sport and their favorite teams.

Basketball's cultural significance is undeniable. It has become interwoven with music, fashion, and entertainment, influencing and being influenced by popular culture trends. Iconic rivalries, memorable teams, and legendary players have all contributed to the sport's unique cultural standing, solidifying its place as a global phenomenon that transcends borders and generations.

Basketball's cultural influence continues to evolve, reflecting societal shifts and technological advancements. Here's a glimpse into how the sport is further embedding itself in the global cultural landscape:

Basketball and Social Activism:

- Athlete Activism: Basketball players are increasingly using their platforms to advocate for social justice, raise awareness about important issues, and inspire change. LeBron James, for example, has been vocal about racial inequality and police brutality, using his influence to promote voter registration and social justice initiatives.
- League-Wide Initiatives: The NBA and WNBA have taken stances on social issues, supporting players' activism and implementing programs to promote diversity, equity, and inclusion. This commitment to

social responsibility further strengthens basketball's cultural relevance and its connection to important societal conversations.

Basketball and Technology:

- Evolving Fan Experiences: Technology is transforming how fans experience basketball, with interactive apps, virtual reality, and augmented reality creating immersive and personalized experiences. These innovations are blurring the lines between the physical and digital worlds, allowing fans to engage with the sport in new and exciting ways.
- Data-Driven Storytelling: Advanced analytics are providing deeper insights into the game, enabling new forms of storytelling and fan engagement. This data-driven approach allows for more personalized content, fantasy sports engagement, and a deeper understanding of player performance.

Basketball and Globalization:

- Cross-Cultural Collaborations: Basketball is facilitating cross-cultural collaborations in music, fashion, and entertainment. International artists, designers, and athletes are collaborating on projects that celebrate basketball's global appeal and its ability to bridge cultural divides.
- Localized Content and Experiences: The NBA is creating localized content and experiences to cater to diverse audiences around the world. This includes broadcasting games in multiple languages, producing region-specific merchandise, and hosting events that celebrate local cultures.

Basketball and the Future:

- The Rise of Women's Basketball: The WNBA is experiencing a surge in popularity, with increased media coverage and growing fan engagement. This

growth reflects a broader cultural shift towards greater gender equality in sports and society.
- Basketball and Esports: The NBA 2K League continues to grow, attracting a new generation of fans and blurring the lines between traditional sports and esports. This convergence of sports and gaming is shaping the future of basketball and its cultural influence.
- Basketball and Social Media: Social media platforms provide a direct connection between athletes and fans, fostering a sense of community and amplifying basketball's cultural impact. Players are using these platforms to build their brands, engage with fans, and express themselves creatively.

Basketball's cultural significance is a dynamic and ever-evolving phenomenon. As the sport continues to grow and adapt to new technologies and societal changes, its influence on music, fashion, entertainment, and social activism will only deepen. Basketball's ability to connect people across cultures and generations ensures its enduring place in the global cultural landscape.

Basketball's cultural narrative continues to unfold, driven by the passion of its fans and the ever-changing landscape of the world:

Basketball as a Tool for Social Commentary:

- Reflecting Societal Issues: Basketball has always been a reflection of society, and today, it serves as a platform for addressing complex issues like social injustice, economic inequality, and mental health. Players, coaches, and leagues are using their voices to spark conversations and inspire change, demonstrating the power of sports to address societal challenges.
- Storytelling Through Film and Documentaries: Filmmakers and documentarians are increasingly using basketball as a lens to explore social issues and tell compelling stories. Documentaries like "The Last

Dance" and "Hoop Dreams" provide insights into the human experience, using basketball as a backdrop to explore themes of race, class, and the pursuit of dreams.

Basketball and the Creative Arts:

- Inspiring Artistic Expression: Basketball's dynamism and artistry have inspired countless works of art, from paintings and sculptures to music and dance. The sport's energy, movement, and emotional intensity provide fertile ground for creative expression.
- Cross-Disciplinary Collaborations: Basketball is increasingly collaborating with other creative disciplines, such as fashion, music, and visual arts. These collaborations result in unique expressions of creativity, blurring the lines between sports and art.

Basketball and Community Building:

- Local Initiatives and Grassroots Programs: Basketball plays a vital role in community building, particularly in underserved areas. Local initiatives and grassroots programs provide safe spaces for young people to play, learn, and develop life skills, fostering a sense of belonging and empowerment.
- Global Community and Fandom: Basketball transcends geographical boundaries, creating a global community of fans who share a passion for the sport. This shared interest fosters connections and friendships, promoting cultural exchange and understanding.

Basketball and Personal Identity:

- Self-Expression and Individuality: Basketball provides a platform for self-expression and individuality. Players develop unique styles of play, and fans express their passion for the sport through fashion, music, and art.
- Role Models and Inspiration: Basketball players often serve as role models, inspiring young people to pursue their dreams and overcome challenges. Their stories of

dedication, perseverance, and achievement resonate with fans around the world.

The Future of Basketball's Cultural Influence:

- Continued Innovation: The NBA and other leagues are constantly innovating, exploring new technologies and formats to engage fans and expand the sport's reach. This commitment to innovation will ensure that basketball remains relevant and exciting for future generations.
- Social Responsibility: Basketball will continue to play a role in social activism and community building, using its platform to address important issues and promote positive change.
- Global Unity: Basketball's universal appeal will continue to bring people together from different backgrounds and cultures, fostering understanding and promoting a shared sense of humanity.

Basketball's cultural influence is a testament to its power to inspire, entertain, and connect people. As the sport continues to evolve, it will undoubtedly remain a vibrant and dynamic force in popular culture, shaping and being shaped by the world around it.

PART 2:

THE LEGENDS OF BASKETBALL

Chapter 1:
BASKETBALL'S EARLY HEROES

These early basketball giants not only dominated the game but also shaped its future, leaving a lasting legacy that continues to inspire generations of players and fans.

Wilt Chamberlain:

- Career: 1959-1973 (Philadelphia/San Francisco Warriors, Philadelphia 76ers, Los Angeles Lakers)
- Major Achievements: 2x NBA Champion, 4x MVP, 13x All-Star, Rookie of the Year, 7x scoring champion, 11x rebounding champion, Hall of Fame
- Playing Style: A physical marvel with unmatched athleticism and strength, Chamberlain revolutionized the center position. His scoring prowess was legendary, including a 100-point game, a record that still stands. He was also a dominant rebounder and defender.
- Legacy: Chamberlain redefined what was possible on the basketball court, pushing the boundaries of athletic achievement. His records and accomplishments remain awe-inspiring, and his impact on the game is undeniable. He paved the way for future dominant centers and inspired generations of players with his incredible skill and athleticism.

Bill Russell:

- Career: 1956-1969 (Boston Celtics)
- Major Achievements: 11x NBA Champion (as a player-coach), 5x MVP, 12x All-Star, Hall of Fame
- Playing Style: Russell was the ultimate winner and defensive anchor. His athleticism, shot-blocking, and

rebounding prowess revolutionized defense in the NBA. He was also a selfless leader and a master of team dynamics.
- Legacy: Russell's impact on basketball transcended statistics. He redefined the importance of defense and teamwork, leading the Boston Celtics to an unprecedented dynasty. His leadership and commitment to winning set a standard for future generations, and his activism off the court made him a cultural icon.

Jerry West:

- Career: 1960-1974 (Los Angeles Lakers)
- Major Achievements: 1x NBA Champion, 14x All-Star, Finals MVP (despite being on the losing team), Hall of Fame, NBA logo
- Playing Style: West was a clutch scorer, a skilled ball-handler, and a fierce competitor. He was known for his all-around excellence and his ability to perform under pressure.
- Legacy: West's competitive spirit and dedication to the game made him one of the most respected players in NBA history. His silhouette graces the NBA logo, forever etching his image into the sport's identity. He was a pioneer of the shooting guard position and an inspiration to countless players.

Influence on the Sport:

These early legends helped shape basketball into the global phenomenon it is today. They:

- Elevated athleticism and skill: They pushed the boundaries of what was possible on the court, inspiring future generations to develop their skills and athleticism.
- Emphasized teamwork and leadership: They demonstrated the importance of teamwork, leadership,

and dedication to winning, setting a standard for future teams and players.
- Expanded the game's popularity: Their captivating performances and captivating personalities drew fans to the sport, contributing to its growth and global reach.
- Inspired future generations: Their legacies continue to inspire young players around the world, demonstrating the power of basketball to achieve greatness and make a difference.

These early basketball legends not only left an indelible mark on the sport but also helped shape its cultural significance. They paved the way for future generations of players and helped establish basketball as a global phenomenon that continues to captivate and inspire millions worldwide.

While Chamberlain, Russell, and West laid the foundation, the story of basketball's legendary figures continued to unfold with new generations of stars who built upon that foundation and added their own unique chapters to the sport's history:

Kareem Abdul-Jabbar:

- Career: 1969-1989 (Milwaukee Bucks, Los Angeles Lakers)
- Major Achievements: 6x NBA Champion, 6x MVP, 19x All-Star, 2x Finals MVP, Hall of Fame
- Playing Style: Known for his unstoppable skyhook, Abdul-Jabbar was a dominant scorer and a graceful athlete. He combined finesse and power, leading the league in scoring twice and becoming the NBA's all-time leading scorer, a record he held for decades.
- Legacy: Abdul-Jabbar's impact extended beyond the court. He was a vocal advocate for social justice and a respected voice in the fight against racial inequality. His enduring legacy includes his athletic achievements, his social activism, and his contributions to basketball's cultural significance.

Oscar Robertson:

- Career: 1960-1974 (Cincinnati Royals, Milwaukee Bucks)
- Major Achievements: 1x NBA Champion, 1x MVP, 12x All-Star, Hall of Fame
- Playing Style: Robertson was a triple-double machine before the term was even coined. He was a complete player, excelling in scoring, passing, and rebounding. His all-around dominance redefined the point guard position.
- Legacy: Robertson's versatility and impact on the game paved the way for future generations of point guards. He was a pioneer of the modern point guard, showcasing the importance of all-around skills and leadership.

Julius Erving ("Dr. J"):

- Career: 1971-1987 (Virginia Squires, New York Nets, Philadelphia 76ers)
- Major Achievements: 1x NBA Champion, 1x ABA Champion, 1x NBA MVP, 3x ABA MVP, 16x All-Star (ABA and NBA), Hall of Fame
- Playing Style: Erving was a high-flying, acrobatic scorer who brought a new level of excitement and athleticism to the game. His dunks and creative moves were ahead of their time, influencing a generation of players.
- Legacy: "Dr. J" was a pioneer of the modern, above-the-rim style of play. His charisma and electrifying moves helped popularize the sport and bridge the gap between the ABA and the NBA.

These legends, along with those mentioned earlier, solidified basketball's position as a major cultural force:

- Media Influence: Their captivating performances were broadcast to wider audiences through television and media coverage, further fueling the sport's popularity.
- Global Impact: Their influence extended beyond the United States, inspiring players and fans around the world.

- Cultural Icons: They became cultural icons, transcending sports and influencing fashion, music, and entertainment.

The stories of these basketball legends continue to inspire and captivate. Their impact on the sport, both on and off the court, helped shape basketball into the global phenomenon it is today, and their legacies continue to be felt in the modern game. Their dedication, skill, and passion for the sport paved the way for future generations of players and fans, ensuring that basketball's rich history and cultural significance will endure for years to come.

As basketball entered the modern era, a new wave of legends emerged, further solidifying the sport's global impact and cultural significance. These players not only dominated the game with their exceptional skills but also captivated audiences with their personalities and charisma:

Magic Johnson:

- Career: 1979-1991, 1996 (Los Angeles Lakers)
- Major Achievements: 5x NBA Champion, 3x MVP, 12x All-Star, 3x Finals MVP, Hall of Fame
- Playing Style: A charismatic showman with exceptional court vision and passing skills, Magic Johnson revolutionized the point guard position. His dazzling no-look passes and infectious smile brought a new level of excitement to the game.
- Legacy: Magic's impact transcended the court. He captivated fans with his joyful style of play and his leadership of the "Showtime" Lakers. His rivalry with Larry Bird revitalized the NBA, and his courageous battle with HIV brought awareness to the disease and inspired millions.

Larry Bird:

- Career: 1979-1992 (Boston Celtics)

- Major Achievements: 3x NBA Champion, 2x Finals MVP, 3x MVP, 12x All-Star, Hall of Fame
- Playing Style: A clutch shooter with exceptional court awareness and a fierce competitive spirit, Larry Bird was a complete player who excelled in all aspects of the game. His trash-talking and intense rivalry with Magic Johnson added another layer of intrigue to the NBA.
- Legacy: Bird's dedication to the game and his relentless pursuit of excellence made him a fan favorite and an inspiration to many. He helped revive the Celtics' winning tradition and contributed to one of the most iconic rivalries in sports history.

Michael Jordan:

- Career: 1984-1993, 1995-1998, 2001-2003 (Chicago Bulls, Washington Wizards)
- Major Achievements: 6x NBA Champion, 6x Finals MVP, 5x MVP, 14x All-Star, Defensive Player of the Year, Hall of Fame
- Playing Style: Considered by many to be the greatest basketball player of all time, Michael Jordan combined athleticism, scoring prowess, and a fierce competitive drive. His gravity-defying dunks, clutch performances, and unwavering determination captivated audiences worldwide.
- Legacy: Jordan's impact on basketball is immeasurable. He transcended the sport, becoming a global icon and a cultural phenomenon. His influence on fashion, music, and entertainment is undeniable, and his legacy continues to inspire athletes and fans around the world.

These modern legends built upon the foundation laid by their predecessors:

- Global Expansion: Their popularity coincided with the NBA's global expansion, further solidifying basketball's international appeal.

- Media and Marketing: They became global brands, endorsing products and appearing in commercials, further embedding basketball into popular culture.
- Social Impact: They used their platforms to address social issues and inspire change, demonstrating the power of athletes to make a difference.

The stories of these basketball legends, along with those who came before and after, continue to shape the sport's narrative. Their influence on the game, its culture, and its global reach is undeniable. They have inspired generations of players and fans, ensuring that basketball's legacy of excellence and cultural significance will endure for years to come.

Chapter 2:
GOLDEN ERA SUPERSTARS

The "Golden Era" of basketball, roughly spanning the 1980s and early 1990s, was a period of unprecedented growth and popularity for the sport. At the heart of this era were three iconic figures who not only dominated the game but also transcended it to become cultural icons:

Larry Bird:

- Career: 1979-1992 (Boston Celtics)
- Memorable Moments:
    - 1981 NBA Finals: Leading the Celtics to victory over the Houston Rockets, showcasing his clutch shooting and all-around excellence.
    - 1986 Eastern Conference Finals: Scoring 29 points in the fourth quarter against the Milwaukee Bucks, a performance that solidified his reputation as a clutch performer.
    - 1984 NBA Finals Game 7: A fierce battle against Magic Johnson and the Lakers, culminating in a Celtics victory and Bird's first Finals MVP award.
- Championships: 3x NBA Champion (1981, 1984, 1986)
- Contributions:
    - Revitalized the Celtics-Lakers rivalry, injecting excitement and passion into the league.
    - Showcased a complete skillset, excelling in scoring, passing, rebounding, and defense.
    - Embodied a blue-collar work ethic and a fierce competitive spirit that resonated with fans.

Magic Johnson:

- Career: 1979-1991, 1996 (Los Angeles Lakers)
- Memorable Moments:
    - 1980 NBA Finals Game 6: Playing center in place of the injured Kareem Abdul-Jabbar and leading the Lakers to victory with a legendary performance.
    - 1987 NBA Finals Game 4: "The Junior, Junior Sky Hook" – a game-winning shot over Kevin McHale and Robert Parish that sealed a crucial victory for the Lakers.
    - Numerous no-look passes and dazzling plays that showcased his exceptional court vision and creativity.
- Championships: 5x NBA Champion (1980, 1982, 1985, 1987, 1988)
- Contributions:
    - Led the "Showtime" Lakers, a team known for its fast-paced, entertaining style of play.
    - Revolutionized the point guard position with his size, passing ability, and leadership.
    - Brought joy and charisma to the game, captivating fans with his infectious smile and positive attitude.

Michael Jordan:

- Career: 1984-1993, 1995-1998, 2001-2003 (Chicago Bulls, Washington Wizards)
- Memorable Moments:
    - 1988 Slam Dunk Contest: His iconic free-throw line dunk that solidified his status as a high-flying superstar.
    - 1991 NBA Finals: "The Shot" – a game-winning jumper over Craig Ehlo in the Eastern Conference Finals, followed by his first NBA Championship.
    - 1998 NBA Finals Game 6: "The Last Shot" – a game-winning jumper over Bryon Russell that

secured his sixth NBA Championship and cemented his legacy.
- Championships: 6x NBA Champion (1991, 1992, 1993, 1996, 1997, 1998)
- Contributions:
  - Elevated the level of athleticism and competitiveness in the NBA.
  - Became a global icon, transcending sports and influencing fashion, music, and popular culture.
  - Inspired countless athletes with his relentless pursuit of excellence and his unwavering determination.

Cultural Influence and Inspiration:

These three legends captivated audiences with their unique personalities and playing styles. They:

- Redefined athleticism and skill: They pushed the boundaries of what was possible on the court, inspiring future generations to strive for greatness.
- Fueled iconic rivalries: Their battles on the court created unforgettable moments and captivated fans, contributing to basketball's cultural significance.
- Became global ambassadors for the sport: Their popularity transcended borders, inspiring athletes and fans worldwide.
- Embodied the spirit of competition and sportsmanship: They exemplified the values of hard work, dedication, and resilience, inspiring future generations to pursue their dreams.

Larry Bird, Magic Johnson, and Michael Jordan were more than just basketball players; they were cultural icons who helped shape the sport's golden era and inspired millions around the world. Their legacies continue to resonate today, reminding us of the power of sports to entertain, inspire, and unite.

The legacy of the golden era extended beyond those iconic names. A constellation of stars emerged, each adding their own unique brilliance to the basketball universe:

Hakeem Olajuwon:

- Career: 1984-2002 (Houston Rockets, Toronto Raptors)
- Memorable Moments:
    - 1994 & 1995 NBA Finals: Leading the Houston Rockets to back-to-back championships with dominant performances against formidable opponents like the New York Knicks and Orlando Magic.
    - "The Dream Shake": His signature footwork and post moves, a mesmerizing blend of finesse and power, left defenders bewildered.
- Championships: 2x NBA Champion (1994, 1995)
- Contributions:
    - Showcased a unique blend of athleticism, grace, and skill in the center position.
    - Inspired a generation of international players, demonstrating the global reach of basketball.
    - Elevated the importance of footwork and post play in the modern game.

Charles Barkley:

- Career: 1984-2000 (Philadelphia 76ers, Phoenix Suns, Houston Rockets)
- Memorable Moments:
    - 1993 NBA Finals: Leading the Phoenix Suns to the Finals with a powerful and passionate performance, though ultimately falling short against Michael Jordan and the Bulls.
    - "The Round Mound of Rebound": His relentless rebounding and physical dominance, defying his relatively smaller stature for a power forward.
- Championships: None (reached the Finals in 1993)
- Contributions:

- - Proved that heart and determination could overcome physical limitations.
  - Became a popular figure for his outspoken personality and entertaining style of play.
  - Added a new dimension to the power forward position with his unique blend of power and agility.

David Robinson:

- Career: 1989-2003 (San Antonio Spurs)
- Memorable Moments:
  - 1999 NBA Finals: Leading the San Antonio Spurs to their first championship with a dominant performance against the New York Knicks.
  - "The Admiral": His exemplary leadership, sportsmanship, and dedication to the game.
- Championships: 2x NBA Champion (1999, 2003)
- Contributions:
  - Anchored the Spurs' dynasty with his defensive prowess and offensive versatility.
  - Exemplified sportsmanship and leadership, earning respect throughout the league.
  - Inspired a generation of players with his commitment to excellence and his dedication to teamwork.

Beyond the Court:

These players, along with their contemporaries, helped solidify basketball's place in popular culture:

- Fashion and Style: Their influence extended to fashion, with signature sneakers and clothing lines becoming popular trends.
- Music and Entertainment: They were featured in music videos, movies, and television shows, further blurring the lines between sports and entertainment.

- Social Activism: They used their platforms to speak out on social issues and inspire change, demonstrating the power of athletes to make a difference.

The golden era of basketball was a time of incredible talent, fierce competition, and cultural impact. The players of this era left an indelible mark on the sport, inspiring generations of athletes and fans and solidifying basketball's place as a global phenomenon. Their legacies continue to inspire and remind us of the power of sports to entertain, unite, and inspire.

As the NBA transitioned into the 21st century, a new generation of stars emerged, carrying the torch passed down by the legends of the golden era. These players continued to push the boundaries of the game, captivating audiences with their incredible athleticism, skill, and personalities:

Shaquille O'Neal:

- Career: 1992-2011 (Orlando Magic, Los Angeles Lakers, Miami Heat, Phoenix Suns, Cleveland Cavaliers, Boston Celtics)
- Memorable Moments:
    - 1995 NBA Finals: Leading the Orlando Magic to the Finals in just his third season, showcasing his dominance and potential.
    - 2000-2002 Three-Peat: Forming a legendary duo with Kobe Bryant and leading the Los Angeles Lakers to three consecutive championships.
    - Shattering backboards: His sheer power and force often led to broken backboards, creating iconic moments that showcased his raw strength.
- Championships: 4x NBA Champion (2000, 2001, 2002, 2006)
- Contributions:
    - Redefined the center position with his combination of size, strength, and agility.
    - Dominated the paint with his powerful dunks and imposing presence.

- Became a larger-than-life personality, entertaining fans with his humor and charisma.

Kobe Bryant:

- Career: 1996-2016 (Los Angeles Lakers)
- Memorable Moments:
  - 2000-2002 Three-Peat: Forming a legendary duo with Shaquille O'Neal and leading the Los Angeles Lakers to three consecutive championships.
  - 2006 81-Point Game: His legendary scoring outburst against the Toronto Raptors, the second-highest single-game point total in NBA history.
  - 2010 NBA Finals Game 7: Leading the Lakers to a dramatic victory over the Boston Celtics, securing his fifth championship and Finals MVP award.
- Championships: 5x NBA Champion (2000, 2001, 2002, 2009, 2010)
- Contributions:
  - Embodied a relentless work ethic and a "Mamba Mentality" that inspired millions.
  - Became a global icon, known for his clutch performances and unwavering determination.
  - Left a lasting legacy of excellence and dedication to the game.

Tim Duncan:

- Career: 1997-2016 (San Antonio Spurs)
- Memorable Moments:
  - 1999 NBA Finals: Leading the San Antonio Spurs to their first championship with a dominant performance against the New York Knicks.
  - 2003 NBA Finals: Winning his second championship and Finals MVP award, solidifying his status as a leader and clutch performer.

- - Consistent excellence throughout his career, earning the nickname "The Big Fundamental" for his fundamentally sound game.
- Championships: 5x NBA Champion (1999, 2003, 2005, 2007, 2014)
- Contributions:
  - Anchored the Spurs' dynasty with his leadership, defense, and consistent play.
  - Exemplified professionalism and teamwork, earning respect throughout the league.
  - Showcased the importance of fundamentals and consistency for long-term success.

Continuing the Legacy:

These players, along with many others, carried the torch from the golden era and continued to shape basketball's cultural impact:

- Global Reach: They expanded the sport's global reach, inspiring new generations of players and fans around the world.
- Social Media Influence: They embraced social media, connecting with fans and building their brands in new ways.
- Social Activism: They used their platforms to advocate for social justice and inspire positive change.

The story of basketball's legends is an ongoing narrative, with each generation adding its own unique contributions to the sport's rich history. These players, with their exceptional talent, dedication, and impact on and off the court, have solidified basketball's place as a global cultural phenomenon. Their legacies continue to inspire and remind us of the power of sports to entertain, unite, and make a difference in the world.

Chapter 3:
MODERN-DAY ICONS

The last 20 years of basketball have been defined by incredible talent and global expansion. Here are some of the icons who have shaped the modern game and continue to inspire:

Kobe Bryant (1996-2016):

- Achievements: 5x NBA Champion, 2x Finals MVP, 1x MVP, 18x All-Star, 2x Olympic Gold Medalist.
- Playing Style: A relentless scorer with a killer instinct, known for his "Mamba Mentality" – a philosophy of hard work, dedication, and unwavering focus. He was a complete offensive player, capable of scoring from anywhere on the court, and a fierce competitor on defense.
- Contributions:
    - Inspired a generation with his work ethic and dedication to excellence.
    - Elevated the global popularity of basketball, particularly in China and other international markets.
    - Bridged the gap between the Jordan era and the modern game.

LeBron James (2003-present):

- Achievements: 4x NBA Champion, 4x Finals MVP, 4x MVP, 19x All-Star, 2x Olympic Gold Medalist.
- Playing Style: A versatile all-around player with exceptional passing ability, court vision, and athleticism. He's often compared to Magic Johnson for his ability to control the game and make his teammates better.
- Contributions:

- Redefined the role of a modern forward with his all-around dominance.
- Used his platform to advocate for social justice and inspire change.
- Continued to push the boundaries of basketball with his longevity and sustained excellence.

Stephen Curry (2009-present):

- Achievements: 4x NBA Champion, 2x MVP, 9x All-Star, 1x Finals MVP.
- Playing Style: A revolutionary shooter who changed the way the game is played with his incredible range and accuracy. He's considered one of the greatest shooters of all time, and his impact on the game is undeniable.
- Contributions:
    - Popularized the three-point shot and ushered in a new era of offensive basketball.
    - Inspired a generation of young players to develop their shooting skills.
    - Demonstrated that skill and finesse can be just as effective as size and strength.

Kevin Durant (2007-present):

- Achievements: 2x NBA Champion, 2x Finals MVP, 1x MVP, 13x All-Star, 2x Olympic Gold Medalist.
- Playing Style: A versatile scorer with exceptional height and length, capable of scoring from anywhere on the court. He's known for his smooth shooting stroke, ball-handling skills, and ability to create his own shot.
- Contributions:
    - Showcased the potential of a modern scorer with his unique blend of size and skill.
    - Embraced new technologies and media platforms to connect with fans.
    - Contributed to the globalization of basketball with his international appeal.

Other Notable Icons:

- Dwyane Wade (2003-2019): A dynamic scorer and fierce competitor, Wade led the Miami Heat to three NBA championships and was known for his acrobatic drives to the basket.
- Dirk Nowitzki (1998-2019): A revolutionary international player, Nowitzki's unique skillset and one-legged fadeaway jumper inspired a generation of European players.
- Giannis Antetokounmpo (2013-present): A physical marvel with incredible athleticism and versatility, Antetokounmpo has led the Milwaukee Bucks to an NBA championship and is considered one of the most dominant players in the league.

Impact and Inspiration:

These modern icons have:

- Elevated the level of play: They have pushed the boundaries of athleticism and skill, inspiring younger players to strive for greatness.
- Expanded global reach: Their popularity has helped basketball become a truly global sport, with fans all over the world.
- Embraced social media: They have used social media to connect with fans, build their brands, and express themselves.
- Used their platforms for good: They have advocated for social justice, promoted education, and inspired positive change.

The legacy of these basketball icons continues to unfold. They are shaping the future of the game and inspiring a new generation of players and fans. Their impact on basketball, both on and off the court, will be felt for years to come.

As basketball continues to evolve, a new generation of stars is emerging, carrying the torch passed down by their predecessors and shaping the future of the game:

Giannis Antetokounmpo (2013-present):

- Achievements: 1x NBA Champion, 1x Finals MVP, 2x MVP, 7x All-Star, Defensive Player of the Year.
- Playing Style: A physical specimen with incredible athleticism, length, and versatility. He dominates both ends of the court with his powerful drives to the basket, ferocious defense, and relentless rebounding.
- Contributions:
    - Redefines the possibilities of a modern forward with his unique combination of size, speed, and skill.
    - Inspires international players with his journey from humble beginnings in Greece to NBA superstardom.
    - Embodies a humble and hardworking attitude that resonates with fans.

Luka Dončić (2018-present):

- Achievements: 4x All-Star.
- Playing Style: A skilled and crafty playmaker with exceptional court vision and scoring ability. He's known for his deceptive moves, step-back jumpers, and ability to control the pace of the game.
- Contributions:
    - Represents the globalization of basketball with his Slovenian heritage and international success.
    - Showcases the importance of skill and basketball IQ in the modern game.
    - Captivates audiences with his creative playmaking and clutch performances.

Nikola Jokić (2015-present):

- Achievements: 2x MVP, 5x All-Star, 1x NBA Champion, 1x Finals MVP.
- Playing Style: A highly skilled center with exceptional passing ability, court awareness, and scoring touch.

He's revolutionizing the center position with his unique blend of size, finesse, and playmaking ability.
- Contributions:
  - Challenges traditional notions of a center with his passing and playmaking skills.
  - Demonstrates the importance of basketball IQ and fundamentals.
  - Inspires international players with his Serbian heritage and NBA success.

Jayson Tatum (2017-present):

- Achievements: 4x All-Star.
- Playing Style: A versatile scorer with a smooth shooting stroke, impressive athleticism, and a growing arsenal of offensive moves. He's developing into a complete player with the potential to become a future superstar.
- Contributions:
  - Represents the next generation of NBA stars with his combination of skill and athleticism.
  - Embraces the legacy of the Boston Celtics and their winning tradition.
  - Inspires young players with his dedication to improvement and his commitment to excellence.

Ja Morant (2019-present):

- Achievements: 2x All-Star, 1x Most Improved Player.
- Playing Style: An explosive and electrifying guard with incredible athleticism, highlight-reel dunks, and fearless drives to the basket. He's known for his high-flying acrobatics and clutch performances.
- Contributions:
  - Brings a new level of excitement and athleticism to the game.
  - Inspires young players with his fearless style of play and his determination to succeed.
  - Represents the future of the point guard position with his unique blend of scoring and playmaking.

Shaping the Future:

These rising stars, along with many other talented players, are shaping the future of basketball:

- Global Impact: They represent a diverse group of players from different backgrounds and nationalities, further expanding the sport's global reach.
- Social Media Influence: They are active on social media, connecting with fans and building their brands in new ways.
- Social Activism: They are using their platforms to advocate for social justice and inspire positive change.

The legacy of basketball's icons continues to evolve with each generation. These players are carrying the torch, pushing the boundaries of the game, and inspiring millions around the world. Their impact on basketball, both on and off the court, will be felt for years to come.

The evolution of basketball continues at a breathtaking pace. Beyond individual players, several trends are shaping the future of the game and its cultural impact:

The Rise of Positionless Basketball:

- Versatility is Key: The traditional roles of guards, forwards, and centers are becoming increasingly blurred. Players like Giannis Antetokounmpo and LeBron James defy traditional positions, excelling in multiple roles and showcasing the importance of versatility in the modern game.
- Emphasis on Skill and IQ: The game is becoming more focused on skill, basketball IQ, and adaptability. Players who can shoot, pass, dribble, and defend effectively, regardless of their size or position, are thriving in this new era.

The Globalization of the Game:

- International Talent: The NBA is becoming increasingly diverse, with players from all over the world showcasing their talents. This influx of international talent is enriching the game and expanding its global reach.
- Growing International Fanbase: Basketball's popularity continues to grow worldwide, with passionate fans in countries like China, the Philippines, and throughout Europe. The NBA is investing in international markets, hosting games and events around the world to connect with this growing fanbase.

The Impact of Technology:

- Advanced Analytics: Data analysis is transforming the way teams scout, train, and strategize. Advanced analytics are providing deeper insights into player performance and game strategy, leading to new levels of efficiency and competition.
- Virtual Reality and Augmented Reality: These technologies are creating immersive experiences for fans, allowing them to feel like they are courtside or even participating in the action. This is revolutionizing fan engagement and opening up new possibilities for training and development.

Social Activism and Social Responsibility:

- Players as Agents of Change: Basketball players are increasingly using their platforms to advocate for social justice, raise awareness about important issues, and inspire positive change. This activism is shaping the cultural conversation and demonstrating the power of athletes to make a difference.
- League-Wide Initiatives: The NBA and other leagues are implementing programs to promote diversity, equity, and inclusion. They are also investing in community initiatives and using their platform to address social issues.

The Future of Basketball:

- Continued Innovation: The NBA is constantly exploring new ways to innovate and engage fans, from experimenting with new game formats to embracing new technologies. This commitment to innovation will ensure that basketball remains exciting and relevant for future generations.
- Social Impact: Basketball will continue to play a role in social activism and community building, using its platform to promote positive change and inspire people around the world.
- Global Growth: The sport's global popularity will continue to grow, with new stars emerging from different corners of the world. Basketball's ability to connect people across cultures and generations ensures its enduring appeal.

The future of basketball is bright, filled with exciting possibilities and driven by the passion of its players and fans. As the game continues to evolve, it will undoubtedly remain a powerful force in sports and culture, inspiring and entertaining millions around the world.

The story of basketball is constantly being written, and the future holds exciting possibilities that will further shape its cultural impact and global reach:

The Rise of Women's Basketball:

- WNBA's Growing Influence: The WNBA continues to gain momentum, showcasing incredible athleticism and skill. Players like Breanna Stewart, A'ja Wilson, and Sue Bird are inspiring a new generation of athletes and challenging traditional gender roles in sports.
- Increased Visibility and Investment: Media coverage of women's basketball is expanding, and investment in the league is growing. This increased visibility is driving fan engagement and creating new opportunities for female athletes to thrive.

Basketball and Social Justice:

- Players as Activists: Basketball players are increasingly using their platforms to advocate for social justice and address systemic inequalities. They are leading conversations about race, gender, and equality, inspiring change and demonstrating the power of sports to impact society.
- League-Wide Initiatives: The NBA and other leagues are actively promoting diversity, equity, and inclusion. They are implementing programs to support social justice initiatives and using their platform to raise awareness about important issues.

Basketball and Entertainment:

- Blurring the Lines: The lines between basketball and entertainment are becoming increasingly blurred. Players are crossing over into music, fashion, and acting, while entertainers are embracing basketball culture and incorporating it into their work.
- New Media and Content Creation: Basketball content is evolving with the rise of new media platforms and digital content creation. Players are building their own brands and connecting with fans through social media, podcasts, and streaming services.

Basketball and Technology:

- Enhanced Fan Experiences: Technology is transforming the fan experience, with virtual reality, augmented reality, and personalized content creating immersive and engaging ways to connect with the game.
- Data-Driven Training and Performance: Advanced analytics and wearable technology are revolutionizing player training and performance optimization. Data-driven insights are helping players improve their skills, prevent injuries, and maximize their potential.

Basketball and Globalization:

- Expanding International Reach: Basketball's global popularity continues to grow, with new leagues and talent emerging in different parts of the world. The NBA is investing in international markets, fostering the growth of the game and connecting with a global fanbase.
- Cultural Exchange and Understanding: Basketball serves as a bridge between cultures, promoting understanding and fostering friendships across borders. The sport's universal appeal transcends language and nationality, bringing people together through a shared passion.

The Future of Basketball:

- Innovation and Adaptation: Basketball will continue to evolve and adapt to new technologies and cultural trends. The game will embrace innovation, explore new formats, and find new ways to engage fans.
- Social Impact: Basketball will continue to play a role in social activism and community building, using its platform to promote positive change and inspire people around the world.
- Global Unity: Basketball will continue to connect people across cultures and generations, fostering a sense of community and shared passion for the game.

The future of basketball is filled with exciting possibilities. As the sport continues to grow and evolve, it will undoubtedly remain a powerful force in sports and culture, inspiring, entertaining, and uniting people around the world.

As we look even further ahead, it's clear that basketball's journey is far from over. The sport continues to evolve, driven by factors both within the game and in the world at large:

Basketball and Social Change:

- Athlete Empowerment: Players are increasingly recognizing their power to effect change beyond the

court. They are becoming vocal advocates for social justice, mental health awareness, and other important causes. This trend empowers athletes to use their platforms to inspire and create a positive impact on society.
- League-Wide Initiatives: Leagues are becoming more proactive in addressing social issues and promoting equality. They are implementing programs to support diversity and inclusion, partnering with organizations that advocate for social change, and using their platform to raise awareness about important causes.

The Intersection of Technology and Basketball:

- Artificial Intelligence (AI): AI is being used to analyze player performance, predict game outcomes, and even personalize fan experiences. AI-powered tools can provide coaches and players with valuable insights to improve training and strategy, while fans can enjoy customized content and interactive experiences.
- Biometrics and Wearable Technology: Wearable technology is providing real-time data on player health and performance, helping to optimize training, prevent injuries, and improve on-court decision-making. This technology is also enhancing fan engagement by providing access to player statistics and personalized insights.

The Evolution of Fan Engagement:

- Immersive Experiences: Virtual reality and augmented reality are creating immersive experiences that bring fans closer to the game than ever before. Fans can experience games from the perspective of their favorite players, participate in virtual training sessions, and interact with other fans in virtual environments.
- Personalized Content: Data analytics and AI are enabling personalized content delivery, tailoring the fan experience to individual preferences. Fans can receive customized game highlights, player-specific news

feeds, and interactive experiences based on their interests.

Basketball as a Global Community:

- Cross-Cultural Collaboration: Basketball is fostering collaboration and understanding across cultures. International players, coaches, and fans are connecting and sharing their passion for the game, breaking down barriers and promoting global citizenship.
- Basketball Diplomacy: The sport is being used as a tool for diplomacy and conflict resolution. Basketball programs and events are bringing people together from different backgrounds, fostering communication and understanding.

The Future of Basketball:

- Sustainability: Leagues and organizations are increasingly focused on sustainability, implementing eco-friendly practices and promoting environmental awareness. This includes initiatives to reduce waste, conserve energy, and promote responsible consumption.
- Accessibility: Efforts are being made to make basketball more accessible to people of all ages, abilities, and backgrounds. This includes initiatives to support adaptive sports programs, provide opportunities for underserved communities, and promote inclusivity.
- Innovation: Basketball will continue to embrace innovation, exploring new technologies, formats, and ways to engage fans. This commitment to innovation will ensure that the sport remains dynamic, exciting, and relevant for future generations.

Basketball's journey is a testament to its enduring appeal and its ability to adapt and evolve. As the sport continues to grow and influence culture, it will undoubtedly remain a powerful force for entertainment, inspiration, and positive change in the world.

Chapter 4:
THE RECORD BREAKERS AND TRAILBLAZERS

Basketball has a rich history of groundbreaking players who have defied expectations, shattered records, and redefined the sport. Here are some of the most influential figures who have left an indelible mark on the game:

Breaking Barriers and Setting New Standards:

- Jackie Robinson (1947): While not a basketball player, Robinson's breaking of the color barrier in Major League Baseball paved the way for integration in all professional sports, including basketball. His courage and perseverance opened doors for African American athletes and changed the face of sports forever.
- Earl Lloyd, Chuck Cooper, and Nat "Sweetwater" Clifton (1950): These three players broke the color barrier in the NBA, paving the way for future generations of African American players. Their entry into the league marked a significant step towards racial integration and equality in professional basketball.

Record-Breaking Pioneers:

- Wilt Chamberlain: Holds numerous NBA records, including scoring 100 points in a single game, a feat unmatched to this day. His dominance and athleticism redefined the center position and pushed the boundaries of what was possible on the court.

- Bill Russell: Won an unprecedented 11 NBA championships with the Boston Celtics, establishing a dynasty and showcasing the importance of defense and teamwork. His impact on the game transcended statistics, as he became a symbol of leadership and social activism.
- Kareem Abdul-Jabbar: The NBA's all-time leading scorer for nearly four decades, Abdul-Jabbar's signature skyhook was virtually unstoppable. He was a dominant force on the court and a vocal advocate for social justice off the court.
- Oscar Robertson: "The Big O" was the first player to average a triple-double for an entire season, showcasing his all-around excellence and redefining the point guard position.

Challenging Norms and Inspiring Change:

- Magic Johnson: His captivating style of play and infectious personality brought a new level of excitement to the game. His courageous battle with HIV raised awareness and challenged stereotypes, inspiring millions around the world.
- Dennis Rodman: Known for his flamboyant personality and unconventional style, Rodman challenged traditional norms and embraced individuality. He was a pioneer in expressing himself both on and off the court, paving the way for greater self-expression in the sport.
- Lisa Leslie: A dominant force in the WNBA, Leslie shattered stereotypes and helped elevate the profile of women's basketball. She was a vocal advocate for gender equality and inspired a generation of female athletes.

Modern Trailblazers:

- Stephen Curry: Revolutionized the game with his incredible three-point shooting, ushering in a new era of offensive basketball and inspiring a generation of players to develop their shooting skills.

- LeBron James: His all-around dominance and longevity have redefined the role of a modern forward. He has also used his platform to advocate for social justice and inspire change, becoming a role model for athletes and fans alike.
- Brittney Griner: A dominant center in the WNBA, Griner has been a vocal advocate for LGBTQ+ rights and has used her platform to raise awareness about social issues.

These players, and many others, have left an indelible mark on basketball, breaking barriers, setting new standards, and inspiring generations of athletes and fans. Their contributions to the game extend beyond the court, as they have used their platforms to challenge norms, promote diversity and inclusion, and make a positive impact on society. Their legacies will continue to shape the future of basketball and inspire future generations to strive for greatness and make a difference in the world.

As basketball continues its journey, it's not just about the players on the court, but the evolving nature of the game itself and its place in society:

The Rise of Advanced Analytics:

- Data-Driven Decision Making: Teams are increasingly relying on advanced analytics to evaluate players, develop game strategies, and make informed decisions. This data-driven approach is revolutionizing the way the game is played and understood.
- Player Tracking and Performance Analysis: Technology is allowing for detailed tracking of player movement and performance, providing valuable insights into individual and team strengths and weaknesses. This data is used to optimize training, prevent injuries, and improve on-court decision-making.

Basketball and Social Consciousness:

- Athlete Activism: Players are becoming more vocal and active in addressing social issues such as racial injustice, gender inequality, and mental health awareness. They are using their platforms to raise awareness, advocate for change, and inspire others to get involved.
- League and Team Initiatives: The NBA and other leagues are taking a more proactive stance on social issues, implementing programs to promote diversity and inclusion, and partnering with organizations to address social challenges.

The Evolution of Basketball Culture:

- Gaming and Esports: The rise of esports and gaming has created new avenues for fans to engage with basketball. Competitive gaming leagues and online communities are fostering a new generation of fans and blurring the lines between virtual and real-world basketball.
- Fashion and Music: Basketball continues to influence fashion and music trends, with players often seen as style icons and musicians incorporating basketball themes into their work. This cross-pollination of cultures further solidifies basketball's place in popular culture.

The Future of Basketball:

- Virtual and Augmented Reality: These technologies are poised to revolutionize the fan experience, creating immersive and interactive ways to engage with the game. Imagine watching a game from the perspective of your favorite player or participating in a virtual training session with a professional athlete.
- Artificial Intelligence: AI will likely play an even greater role in the future of basketball, from scouting and player development to game analysis and fan engagement. AI-powered tools could personalize the fan experience, provide real-time insights during games, and even assist with coaching and training.

- Global Expansion: Basketball's popularity will continue to grow globally, with new talent emerging from different parts of the world. The NBA and other leagues will continue to invest in international markets, fostering the growth of the game and connecting with a global fanbase.

Basketball's journey is a testament to its adaptability and enduring appeal. As the sport continues to evolve, it will undoubtedly remain a powerful force in sports and culture, inspiring, entertaining, and uniting people around the world. The future of basketball is bright, filled with exciting possibilities and driven by the passion of its players, fans, and the ever-changing world around it.

As basketball hurtles towards the future, its story continues to unfold in exciting and unexpected ways. Here are some emerging trends and potential developments that could further shape the game:

Basketball and the Metaverse:

- Virtual Worlds and Immersive Experiences: Imagine attending a virtual NBA game from the comfort of your home, interacting with other fans in a virtual arena, and even owning digital collectibles related to your favorite players and teams. The metaverse offers exciting possibilities for basketball to create immersive fan experiences and expand its reach into new digital frontiers.
- New Revenue Streams and Fan Engagement: The metaverse could open up new revenue streams for teams and players through virtual merchandise, digital collectibles, and interactive experiences. It could also provide new ways for fans to engage with the game, participate in virtual events, and connect with other fans around the world.

The Rise of Alternative Leagues:

- Challenging the Status Quo: New basketball leagues and competitions are emerging, challenging the traditional structures and offering alternative pathways for players and fans. These leagues could experiment with new rules, formats, and technologies, potentially driving innovation and pushing the boundaries of the sport.
- Expanding Opportunities: Alternative leagues could provide opportunities for players who may not fit the traditional mold or who are seeking different paths to professional basketball. They could also create new avenues for fans to engage with the game and support different styles of play.

Basketball and Social Impact:

- Mental Health Awareness: The conversation surrounding mental health in sports is gaining momentum. Players are becoming more open about their struggles, and leagues are implementing programs to support mental wellness. This focus on mental health could help destigmatize the issue and create a more supportive environment for athletes.
- Environmental Sustainability: Basketball is increasingly recognizing its responsibility to address environmental concerns. Leagues and teams are implementing sustainable practices, reducing their carbon footprint, and promoting environmental awareness among players and fans.

The Evolution of Coaching and Player Development:

- Data-Driven Coaching: Advanced analytics and AI are transforming coaching strategies and player development. Coaches are using data to personalize training programs, optimize game plans, and identify areas for improvement.
- Emphasis on Holistic Development: Player development is increasingly focusing on holistic well-being, encompassing physical, mental, and emotional

aspects. This approach recognizes the importance of supporting athletes both on and off the court, fostering their overall growth and development.

The Future of Basketball:

- Increased Inclusivity: Basketball will continue to strive for greater inclusivity, creating opportunities for people of all ages, abilities, and backgrounds to participate and enjoy the game. This includes supporting adaptive sports programs, promoting gender equality, and fostering diversity at all levels of the sport.
- Technological Integration: Technology will continue to play a significant role in the evolution of basketball, from enhancing fan experiences to improving player performance and driving innovation in the game.
- Global Community: Basketball will continue to connect people across cultures and continents, fostering a sense of global community and shared passion for the game.

The future of basketball is filled with possibilities. As the sport continues to evolve, it will undoubtedly remain a powerful force in sports and culture, inspiring, entertaining, and uniting people around the world. By embracing innovation, promoting social responsibility, and fostering inclusivity, basketball can continue to grow and thrive for generations to come.

As basketball continues its dynamic journey, several emerging trends and potential developments are poised to shape its future and further solidify its position as a global cultural phenomenon:

The Rise of Personalized Basketball Experiences:

- AI-Powered Training and Analysis: Artificial intelligence and machine learning will play an even greater role in player development. Imagine AI-powered systems that analyze individual playing styles, identify areas for

improvement, and create personalized training programs tailored to each player's needs and goals.
- Customized Fan Engagement: AI could also revolutionize fan engagement by delivering personalized content and experiences. Imagine receiving customized game highlights, player-specific news feeds, and interactive experiences based on your individual preferences and viewing habits.

Basketball and the Creator Economy:

- Player Empowerment and Brand Building: Players are increasingly leveraging social media and digital platforms to build their own brands and connect directly with fans. This trend empowers athletes to control their own narratives, express their individuality, and create new revenue streams.
- Content Creation and Storytelling: Basketball players are becoming content creators, sharing their stories, insights, and experiences through various media. This trend is blurring the lines between athletes and entertainers, offering fans a more intimate and engaging connection with the game.

The Evolution of Basketball Analytics:

- Real-Time Data and In-Game Insights: Advanced analytics will provide real-time data and insights during games, enhancing the viewing experience for fans and providing coaches with valuable information to make strategic adjustments.
- Predictive Analytics and Player Evaluation: AI-powered predictive analytics could revolutionize scouting and player evaluation, identifying potential stars and predicting future performance with greater accuracy.

Basketball and Social Responsibility:

- Mental Health Advocacy: The conversation surrounding mental health in sports will continue to evolve, with

greater emphasis on supporting athletes' mental well-being and destigmatizing mental health challenges.
- Environmental Sustainability: Basketball leagues and organizations will continue to prioritize sustainability, implementing eco-friendly practices, reducing their carbon footprint, and promoting environmental awareness among players and fans.

The Future of Basketball:

- Increased Accessibility: Efforts to make basketball more accessible to people of all ages, abilities, and backgrounds will continue. This includes promoting adaptive sports programs, creating opportunities for underserved communities, and fostering inclusivity at all levels of the game.
- Technological Innovation: Technology will continue to drive innovation in basketball, from enhancing fan experiences to improving player performance and creating new ways to engage with the game.
- Global Community: Basketball will continue to connect people across cultures and continents, fostering a sense of global community and shared passion for the game.

The future of basketball is filled with promise and potential. As the sport continues to evolve, it will undoubtedly remain a vibrant and influential force in sports and culture, inspiring, entertaining, and uniting people around the world. By embracing innovation, promoting social responsibility, and fostering inclusivity, basketball can continue to thrive and leave a lasting legacy for generations to come.

As basketball continues its journey, it's not just about the players on the court, but the evolving nature of the game itself and its place in society:

The Rise of Advanced Analytics:

- Data-Driven Decision Making: Teams are increasingly relying on advanced analytics to evaluate players, develop game strategies, and make informed decisions. This data-driven approach is revolutionizing the way the game is played and understood.
- Player Tracking and Performance Analysis: Technology is allowing for detailed tracking of player movement and performance, providing valuable insights into individual and team strengths and weaknesses. This data is used to optimize training, prevent injuries, and improve on-court decision-making.

Basketball and Social Consciousness:

- Athlete Activism: Players are becoming more vocal and active in addressing social issues such as racial injustice, gender inequality, and mental health awareness. They are using their platforms to raise awareness, advocate for change, and inspire others to get involved.
- League and Team Initiatives: The NBA and other leagues are taking a more proactive stance on social issues, implementing programs to promote diversity and inclusion, and partnering with organizations to address social challenges.

The Evolution of Basketball Culture:

- Gaming and Esports: The rise of esports and gaming has created new avenues for fans to engage with basketball. Competitive gaming leagues and online communities are fostering a new generation of fans and blurring the lines between virtual and real-world basketball.
- Fashion and Music: Basketball continues to influence fashion and music trends, with players often seen as style icons and musicians incorporating basketball themes into their work. This cross-pollination of cultures further solidifies basketball's place in popular culture.

The Future of Basketball:

- Virtual and Augmented Reality: These technologies are poised to revolutionize the fan experience, creating immersive and interactive ways to engage with the game. Imagine watching a game from the perspective of your favorite player or participating in a virtual training session with a professional athlete.
- Artificial Intelligence: AI will likely play an even greater role in the future of basketball, from scouting and player development to game analysis and fan engagement. AI-powered tools could personalize the fan experience, provide real-time insights during games, and even assist with coaching and training.
- Global Expansion: Basketball's popularity will continue to grow globally, with new talent emerging from different parts of the world. The NBA and other leagues will continue to invest in international markets, fostering the growth of the game and connecting with a global fanbase.

Basketball's journey is a testament to its adaptability and enduring appeal. As the sport continues to evolve, it will undoubtedly remain a powerful force in sports and culture, inspiring, entertaining, and uniting people around the world. The future of basketball is bright, filled with exciting possibilities and driven by the passion of its players, fans, and the ever-changing world around it.

PART 3:

INTERACTIVE GAMES & CHALLENGES

Chapter 1:
TRUE-FALSE SECTION

1. Basketball was invented in the United States.
2. The first basketballs were brown.
3. The NBA was founded in the 1950s.
4. Wilt Chamberlain holds the record for the most rebounds in a single game.
5. Bill Russell won 11 NBA championships with the Los Angeles Lakers.
6. The "Dream Team" refers to the 1992 USA Olympic men's basketball team.
7. A free throw is worth 2 points.
8. A player can hold the ball for 10 seconds before dribbling, passing, or shooting.
9. A shot made from outside the three-point line is worth 3 points.
10. The WNBA was founded in 1997.
11. Lisa Leslie holds the record for the most points scored in WNBA history.
12. The Harlem Globetrotters are known for their comedic basketball skills.
13. The shot clock in the NBA is 30 seconds.
14. Traveling is a violation that occurs when a player takes too many steps without dribbling the ball.

15. A double dribble occurs when a player dribbles the ball with two hands simultaneously.
16. A technical foul is called when a player commits a personal foul.
17. The NBA Finals is a best-of-seven series.
18. The first basketball game was played outdoors.
19. The term "slam dunk" was coined by Red Auerbach.
20. Shaquille O'Neal played for the Orlando Magic and the Los Angeles Lakers, among other teams.
21. Larry Bird played his entire career for the Boston Celtics.
22. Magic Johnson and Larry Bird were teammates in the 1980s.
23. The 3-point line was introduced to the NBA in 1985.
24. Michael Jordan wore the number 23 throughout his entire NBA career.
25. LeBron James was drafted directly out of college.
26. Stephen Curry is known for his exceptional three-point shooting.
27. The NBA All-Star Game features the best players from the Eastern Conference against the best players from the Western Conference.
28. The NBA MVP award is given to the best player in the NBA Finals.

29. The term "triple-double" refers to a player recording double digits in three statistical categories in a single game.
30. Bill Russell won 13 NBA championships with the Boston Celtics.
31. The "shot clock" violation occurs when a player fails to shoot the ball before the shot clock expires.
32. A "flagrant foul" is a personal foul that involves excessive or violent contact.
33. The "goaltending" rule prohibits players from touching the ball while it is on its upward trajectory toward the basket.
34. The term "assist" refers to a pass that directly leads to a made basket.
35. The "backcourt violation" occurs when a player dribbles the ball from the backcourt to the frontcourt.
36. The "zone defense" is a defensive strategy where each player guards a specific opponent.
37. The "man-to-man defense" is a defensive strategy where each player guards a specific area of the court.
38. The term "fast break" refers to a slow offensive transition after a turnover or rebound.
39. The "pick and roll" is an offensive play involving a screen set by one player for a teammate.
40. The original basketball hoops were open at the bottom.
41. Basketball was introduced to the Olympics in 1936.

42. The Women's National Basketball Association (WNBA) is the leading professional women's basketball league in the world.
43. The Naismith Memorial Basketball Hall of Fame is located in Boston, Massachusetts.
44. The term "air ball" refers to a shot that completely misses the rim and backboard.
45. A player can be called for traveling if they jump and land with the ball without dribbling.
46. The term "alley-oop" refers to a high pass that is caught and dunked in one motion.
47. The "Euro step" is a move where a player takes a step in one direction, then another step in the same direction to avoid a defender.
48. The "and-one" occurs when a player makes a basket while being fouled and gets a chance for a free throw.
49. The NBA has a salary cap, which limits the amount of money teams can spend on player salaries.
50. The term "sixth man" refers to the sixth player on the starting lineup.
51. A player can be called for a foul if they block a shot after it has hit the backboard.
52. The "paint" refers to the circular area on the court around the basket.
53. The term "triple threat position" refers to a player holding the ball with the ability to shoot, pass, or dribble.

54. The "charge" is an offensive foul that occurs when a defensive player runs into an offensive player who has established a legal guarding position.
55. The term "flopping" refers to a player exaggerating contact to draw a foul.
56. The "draft lottery" is a system used to determine the order of selection in the NBA draft.
57. The term "rookie" refers to a player in their second year in the NBA.
58. The "trade deadline" is the date after which NBA teams can no longer make trades.
59. The term "free agency" refers to the period when NBA players can only sign with their current team.
60. The term "swingman" refers to a player who can play both the center and power forward positions.
61. The "postseason" refers to the regular season games that occur before the playoffs.
62. The term "buzzer beater" refers to a shot made just after the game clock expires.
63. The "traveling violation" can also be called if a player moves their pivot foot.
64. The "offensive rebound" occurs when a defensive player grabs a missed shot.
65. The "defensive rebound" occurs when a defensive player grabs a missed shot by the opposing team.

66. The term "box out" refers to a player using their body to position themselves for a rebound.
67. The term "turnover" refers to when a team gains possession of the ball.
68. The "inbound pass" is a pass thrown from out of bounds to restart play.
69. The "jump ball" is a method used to start the second half of the game.
70. The "possession arrow" is used to determine which team gets possession of the ball after a made basket.
71. A player can score a basket directly from an inbound pass.
72. The term "screen" refers to a player illegally obstructing a defender's path.
73. The term "give-and-go" refers to a player passing the ball to a teammate and then immediately cutting to the basket to receive a return pass.
74. A player can be called for a foul if they reach in and make contact with the ball handler's arm.
75. The term "palming" refers to a player legally carrying the ball while dribbling.
76. The "bonus" situation occurs when a team has committed a certain number of fouls in a quarter, resulting in the opposing team shooting free throws for each subsequent foul.

77. The term "double bonus" refers to a situation where a team shoots three free throws for each non-shooting foul committed by the opposing team.
78. The term "ejection" refers to a player being removed from the game for committing a common foul.
79. The "shot clock" resets to 24 seconds after an offensive rebound.
80. The term "backdoor cut" refers to an offensive player cutting behind the defense towards the basket.
81. The term "cherry-picking" refers to a player staying near their own basket while their team is on offense.
82. The term "coast-to-coast" refers to a player dribbling the ball the full length of the court for a score.
83. The term "crossover dribble" refers to a player bouncing the ball from one hand to the other.
84. The term "fadeaway" refers to a player leaning backwards while shooting a jump shot.
85. The term "hook shot" refers to a player shooting the ball with one hand in a sweeping motion.
86. The term "isolation" refers to an offensive play where a player is isolated against a single defender.
87. The term "no-look pass" refers to a player passing the ball without looking at the receiver.
88. The term "posterize" refers to a player dunking over a defender in a spectacular fashion.

89. The term "putback" refers to a player grabbing an offensive rebound and immediately scoring.
90. The term "swingman" refers to a player who can play both guard and forward positions.
91. The term "transition" refers to the shift from offense to defense or defense after a made basket or turnover.
92. The term "traveling" refers to a player taking too many steps without dribbling the ball.
93. The term "double dribble" refers to a player dribbling the ball, stopping, and then dribbling again.
94. The term "technical foul" refers to a foul called for unsportsmanlike conduct or violations of rules.
95. The term "flagrant foul" refers to a personal foul that involves excessive or violent contact.
96. The term "goaltending" refers to a player illegally interfering with a shot while it is in the air.
97. The term "alley-oop" refers to a high pass that is caught and dunked in one motion.
98. The term "and-one" refers to a player making a basket while being fouled and getting a chance for a free throw.
99. The term "buzzer beater" refers to a shot made just before the game clock expires.
100. The term "triple-double" refers to a player recording double-digits in three statistical categories in a single game.

Answers

1. False. Basketball was invented in Canada.
2. True.
3. False. It was founded in 1946.
4. True.
5. False. Bill Russell won 11 NBA championships with the Boston Celtics.
6. True.
7. False. A free throw is worth 1 point.
8. False. A player can only hold the ball for 2 seconds without dribbling.
9. True.
10. True.
11. False. Diana Taurasi holds that record.
12. True.
13. False. The shot clock in the NBA is 24 seconds.
14. True.
15. True.
16. False. A technical foul is called for unsportsmanlike conduct.
17. True.
18. False. The first game was played indoors.
19. False. Chick Hearn coined the term.
20. True.
21. True.

22. False. They were rivals.
23. False. It was introduced in 1979.
24. False. He briefly wore number 45.
25. False. He was drafted out of high school.
26. True.
27. True.
28. False. It is given to the best player in the regular season.
29. True.
30. False. He won 11 championships.
31. True.
32. True.
33. False. It prohibits touching the ball on its downward trajectory.
34. True.
35. False. It occurs when a player dribbles from the frontcourt to the backcourt.
36. False. Zone defense guards an area.
37. False. Man-to-man defense guards a player.
38. False. It refers to a quick offensive transition.
39. True.
40. False. They were closed at the bottom.
41. True.
42. True.
43. False. It is located in Springfield, Massachusetts.
44. True.

45. True.
46. True.
47. False. The Euro step involves stepping in opposite directions.
48. True.
49. True.
50. False. The sixth man comes off the bench.
51. False. Goaltending only applies to a shot on its downward trajectory.
52. False. The paint is rectangular.
53. True.
54. False. It is a defensive foul.
55. True.
56. True.
57. False. A rookie is in their first year.
58. True.
59. False. Players can sign with any team during free agency.
60. False. A swingman plays both guard positions.
61. False. The postseason refers to the playoffs.
62. False. A buzzer-beater is made before the clock expires.
63. True.
64. False. An offensive rebound is grabbed by an offensive player.
65. True.

66. True.
67. False. A turnover is losing possession.
68. True.
69. False. A jump ball starts the game and overtime.
70. False. The possession arrow is used after a held ball.
71. True.
72. False. A screen is a legal obstruction.
73. True.
74. True.
75. False. Palming is illegally carrying the ball.
76. True.
77. False. The double bonus is two free throws.
78. False. An ejection is for a serious foul or two technicals.
79. False. The shot clock is usually shorter after an offensive rebound.
80. True.
81. True.
82. True.
83. True.
84. True.
85. True.
86. True.
87. True.
88. True.
89. True.
90. True.

91. True.
92. True.
93. True.
94. True.
95. True.
96. True.
97. True.
98. True.
99. True.
100. True.

Chapter 2:
PLAYER AND COURT QUESTIONS

1. **Who holds the record for the most career assists in the NBA?**

    a) Magic Johnson

    b) Jason Kidd

    c) Chris Paul

    d) John Stockton

2. **Which country won the first-ever Olympic gold medal in basketball?**

    a) United States

    b) Soviet Union

    c) Yugoslavia

    d) Argentina

3. **What is the term for a player who can play both guard and forward positions?**

    a) Center

    b) Power forward

c) Swingman

d) Point guard

4. **Which player is known for his signature "finger roll" layup?**

   a) George Gervin

   b) Kareem Abdul-Jabbar

   c) Wilt Chamberlain

   d) Hakeem Olajuwon

5. **What is the name of the famous outdoor basketball court in Paris, France?**

   a) Rucker Park

   b) Venice Beach Courts

   c) Quai 54

   d) The Cage

6. **Which player is known for his signature "Dream Shake" move?**

   a) Shaquille O'Neal

   b) Hakeem Olajuwon

   c) Tim Duncan

   d) David Robinson

7. What is the term for a defensive strategy where each player guards a specific area of the court?

   a) Man-to-man defense

   b) Zone defense

   c) Full-court press

   d) Double team

8. Which player is nicknamed "Agent Zero"?

   a) Gilbert Arenas

   b) Carmelo Anthony

   c) Tracy McGrady

   d) Vince Carter

9. What is the name of the famous basketball arena in Los Angeles, California?

   a) Madison Square Garden

   b) Staples Center (now Crypto.com Arena)

   c) United Center

   d) TD Garden

10. Which player is known for his signature one-handed "tomahawk" dunk?

    a) Dominique Wilkins

    b) Darryl Dawkins

c) Vince Carter

d) Blake Griffin

11. What is the term for a violation that occurs when a player dribbles the ball with two hands simultaneously?

   a) Traveling

   b) Double dribble

   c) Carrying

   d) Palming

12. Which player is nicknamed "The Black Mamba"?

   a) Kobe Bryant

   b) Michael Jordan

   c) LeBron James

   d) Kevin Durant

13. What is the name of the famous basketball movie starring Michael Jordan and Bugs Bunny?

   a) Hoosiers

   b) Space Jam

   c) White Men Can't Jump

   d) Coach Carter

14. Which player is known for his signature "Euro step" move?

   a) Manu Ginobili

   b) Dirk Nowitzki

   c) Tony Parker

   d) Pau Gasol

15. What is the term for a foul called on a player who impedes the progress of an opponent without making contact with the ball?

   a) Blocking foul

   b) Charging foul

   c) Personal foul

   d) Technical foul

16. Which player is nicknamed "The Beard"?

   a) James Harden

   b) Stephen Curry

   c) Klay Thompson

   d) Damian Lillard

17. What is the name of the famous basketball video game series?

   a) Madden NFL

b) FIFA

c) NBA 2K

d) NHL

18. Which player is known for his signature "no-look pass"?

   a) Magic Johnson

   b) Larry Bird

   c) Jason Kidd

   d) Steve Nash

19. What is the term for an offensive play where a player sets a screen for a teammate and then rolls to the basket?

   a) Pick and roll

   b) Give-and-go

   c) Isolation

   d) Post-up

20. Which player is nicknamed "King James"?

   a) LeBron James

   b) Michael Jordan

   c) Kareem Abdul-Jabbar

   d) Bill Russell

21. Which player is known for shattering backboards with his powerful dunks?

   a) Shaquille O'Neal

   b) Darryl Dawkins

   c) Blake Griffin

   d) Dwight Howard

22. What is the term for an offensive player cutting towards the basket from the weak side of the court?

   a) Backdoor cut

   b) Pick and roll

   c) Give-and-go

   d) Alley-oop

23. Which player is nicknamed "The Claw" for his defensive skills?

   a) Kawhi Leonard

   b) Dennis Rodman

   c) Gary Payton

   d) Scottie Pippen

24. What is the name of the basketball hall of fame located in Springfield, Massachusetts?

   a) Naismith Memorial Basketball Hall of Fame

b) National Baseball Hall of Fame and Museum

c) Pro Football Hall of Fame

d) Hockey Hall of Fame

25. **Which player is known for his signature "between-the-legs" dribble move?**

    a) Allen Iverson

    b) Jason Williams

    c) Kyrie Irving

    d) Jamal Crawford

26. **What is the term for a player intentionally exaggerating contact to draw a foul?**

    a) Flopping

    b) Charging

    c) Blocking

    d) Traveling

27. **Which player is nicknamed "The Greek Freak"?**

    a) Giannis Antetokounmpo

    b) Luka Dončić

    c) Nikola Jokić

    d) Domantas Sabonis

28. What is the name of the rule that prohibits offensive players from remaining in the free throw lane for more than three seconds?

   a) Three-second violation

   b) Five-second violation

   c) Eight-second violation

   d) Ten-second violation

29. Which player is nicknamed "Chef Curry" for his incredible shooting ability?

   a) Stephen Curry

   b) Klay Thompson

   c) Ray Allen

   d) Reggie Miller

30. What is the term for a situation where a team has committed a certain number of fouls in a quarter, resulting in the opposing team shooting free throws for each subsequent foul?

   a) Bonus

   b) Double bonus

   c) Technical foul

   d) Flagrant foul

31. How many periods are there in an NBA game?

32. How long is each quarter in an NBA game?
33. What is the term for the area on the court between the free throw line and the baseline?
34. How many timeouts can each team take in an NBA game?
35. What is the term for a shot that hits the rim and bounces back into play?
36. What is the term for a player grabbing a missed shot by their own team?
37. What is the term for a player illegally gaining possession of the ball by pushing or holding an opponent?
38. Who won the NBA championship in 2023?
39. Who is the head coach of the Milwaukee Bucks?
40. Who is the head coach of the Philadelphia 76ers?
41. Which team did Larry Bird play for his entire career?
42. Which team did Magic Johnson play for his entire career?
43. Who is the all-time leader in three-pointers made in NBA history?
44. Who is the youngest player to score 10,000 points in the NBA?
45. Who is the only player to win the NBA MVP, Finals MVP, and Defensive Player of the Year awards in the same season?

46. Who is the only player to win five NBA championships with two different teams?
47. What is the name of the NBA's developmental league?
48. Who won the WNBA championship in 2023?
49. Who is the head coach of the New York Liberty?
50. Who is the head coach of the Connecticut Sun?
51. What is the name of the international basketball federation?
52. Who is the current president of FIBA?
53. In what year was the 3-point line introduced to the NBA?
54. What is the distance of the NBA 3-point line?
55. What is the name of the first professional basketball league in the United States?
56. Who is credited with inventing the jump shot?
57. What is the name of the first African American player in the NBA?
58. Who was the first woman to play in an NBA game?
59. What is the name of the award given to the best defensive player in the NBA?
60. What is the name of the award given to the player who shows the most improvement during the NBA season?
61. What is the minimum number of players a team must have to start an NBA game?
62. What is the term for a pass thrown from out of bounds to restart play?

63. What is the term for a method used to start the game and overtime periods?
64. What is the term for a situation where two opposing players have simultaneous possession of the ball?
65. What is the term for the arrow used to determine which team gets possession of the ball after a held ball situation?
66. What is the maximum number of personal fouls a player can commit in an NBA game before being disqualified?
67. What is the term for a player being removed from the game for committing a serious foul or receiving two technical fouls?
68. What is the term for the period when NBA players can sign with any team?
69. What is the term for the date after which NBA teams can no longer make trades?
70. What is the name of the award given to the best rookie in the NBA?
71. What is the name of the award given to the best sixth man in the NBA?
72. What is the name of the award given to the coach of the year in the NBA?
73. What is the name of the award given to the executive of the year in the NBA?
74. What is the name of the first openly gay active player in the NBA?

75. Who was the first player to be drafted number one overall directly out of high school?
76. Which two teams played in the longest NBA game in history?
77. What was the final score of the longest NBA game in history?
78. Which team holds the record for the most consecutive NBA championships?
79. What is the name of the first player to score over 30,000 points in the NBA?
80. Who is the only NBA player to average a triple-double for an entire season?

Answers

1. d) John Stockton - He holds the record with 15,806 career assists.
2. a) United States - They defeated Canada in the final in 1936.
3. c) Swingman
4. a) George Gervin - Known as "The Iceman" for his smooth moves.
5. c) Quai 54 - A popular outdoor tournament held annually in Paris.
6. b) Hakeem Olajuwon - His signature footwork move was nearly unstoppable.
7. b) Zone defense
8. a) Gilbert Arenas - Known for his scoring outbursts and clutch performances.
9. b) Staples Center (now Crypto.com Arena) - Home to the Lakers and Clippers.
10. a) Dominique Wilkins - Known as "The Human Highlight Film" for his powerful dunks.
11. b) Double dribble
12. a) Kobe Bryant - He adopted the nickname to represent his killer instinct on the court.
13. b) Space Jam
14. a) Manu Ginobili - He popularized the move in the NBA.
15. a) Blocking foul

16. a) James Harden - Known for his prolific scoring and signature beard.
17. c) NBA 2K
18. a) Magic Johnson - His court vision and passing skills were legendary.
19. a) Pick and roll
20. a) LeBron James
21. b) Darryl Dawkins - He was known as "Chocolate Thunder" for his powerful dunks that broke backboards.
22. a) Backdoor cut
23. a) Kawhi Leonard - His large hands and defensive prowess earned him this nickname.
24. a) Naismith Memorial Basketball Hall of Fame
25. b) Jason Williams - "White Chocolate" was known for his flashy style.
26. a) Flopping
27. a) Giannis Antetokounmpo - From Greece, he's known for his incredible athleticism and versatility.
28. a) Three-second violation
29. a) Stephen Curry - His incredible shooting range and accuracy have revolutionized the game.
30. a) Bonus
31. 4 periods (quarters)
32. 12 minutes
33. The paint (also known as the key or the lane)
34. 7 timeouts (including 1 coach's challenge)

35. Rebound
36. Offensive rebound
37. Holding
38. Denver Nuggets
39. Adrian Griffin
40. Nick Nurse
41. Boston Celtics
42. Los Angeles Lakers
43. Stephen Curry
44. LeBron James
45. Michael Jordan (1988)
46. Michael Jordan (Chicago Bulls and Washington Wizards)
47. NBA G League
48. Las Vegas Aces
49. Sandy Brondello
50. Stephanie White
51. FIBA (International Basketball Federation)
52. Hamane Niang
53. 1979
54. 23 feet 9 inches (from the center of the basket)
55. National Basketball League (NBL) (founded in 1898)
56. Glenn Roberts (though others also contributed to its development)
57. Earl Lloyd
58. Nancy Lieberman (in an exhibition game)

59. Kia NBA Defensive Player of the Year Award
60. Kia NBA Most Improved Player Award
61. 5 players
62. Inbound pass
63. Jump ball
64. Held ball
65. Possession arrow
66. 6 fouls
67. Ejection
68. Free agency
69. Trade deadline
70. Kia NBA Rookie of the Year Award
71. Kia NBA Sixth Man of the Year Award
72. Michael H. Goldberg NBCA Coach of the Year Award
73. NBA Executive of the Year Award
74. Jason Collins
75. Kwame Brown (drafted by the Washington Wizards in 2001)
76. Indianapolis Olympians and Rochester Royals (played on January 6, 1951)
77. 75-73 (Rochester Royals won in six overtimes)
78. Boston Celtics (won 8 consecutive championships from 1959 to 1966)
79. Wilt Chamberlain
80. Russell Westbrook (achieved this feat in the 2016-17, 2017-18, and 2018-19 seasons)

Chapter 3:
ADVANCED TRIVIA CHALLENGES

1. What is the "transition take foul" rule, and why was it introduced?
2. Explain the difference between a "loose ball foul" and a "reach-in foul."
3. What is the "ten-second violation" in basketball, and when does it apply?
4. What is the "lower defensive box" in basketball, and how does it relate to defensive three-second violations?
5. Describe the "jump ball" procedure and how it has evolved over the years.
6. What is the "strong side" in basketball, and how does it influence offensive and defensive strategies?
7. Explain the concept of "defensive three seconds" and its purpose in the NBA.
8. What is an "unsportsmanlike foul," and how is it different from a "technical foul"?
9. Describe the "double dribble" rule and the various ways players can violate it.
10. What is the "penalty" situation in basketball, and how does it differ from the "bonus" situation?

11. What is the difference between a "personal foul" and a "common foul"?
12. Explain the "basket interference" rule and how it applies to both offensive and defensive players.
13. What is the "shot clock reset" rule, and how can it vary depending on different leagues and situations?
14. What is a "quadruple-double" in basketball, and who are some players who have achieved it?
15. Explain the concept of "team fouls" in basketball and how they impact the game.
16. What is a "traveling violation" during a free throw attempt?
17. What is an "illegal screen" in basketball, and what makes a screen legal?
18. Explain the "backcourt violation" in basketball and the exceptions to this rule.
19. What is the "offensive basket interference" rule?
20. What is a "held ball" violation in basketball, and how is it different from a "jump ball" situation?
21. In what year was the WNBA founded?
22. What is the name of the basketball league in which Magic Johnson and Larry Bird played their iconic rivalry?
23. Who is credited with coining the term "March Madness"?

24. What is the name of the first woman to coach an NBA team?
25. Who was the shortest player to ever play in the NBA?
26. Which NBA team holds the record for the most wins in a single season?
27. Who is the only player to win three consecutive NBA Finals MVP awards with three different teams?
28. What is the name of the award given to the most valuable player in the NBA All-Star Game?
29. What is the name of the award given to the player with the best sportsmanship in the NBA?
30. What is the name of the award given to the best teammate in the NBA?
31. What is the name of the first basketball video game?
32. Who was the first player to be inducted into the Naismith Memorial Basketball Hall of Fame?
33. In what year did women's basketball become an official Olympic sport?
34. What is the name of the first basketball shoe endorsed by Michael Jordan?
35. What is the name of the first basketball team to win back-to-back NBA championships?
36. Who is the youngest player to ever be drafted into the NBA?
37. What is the name of the oldest professional basketball league in the world still in operation?

38. Who is the only player to win an NBA championship, an NCAA championship, and an Olympic gold medal in the same year?
39. What is the name of the award given to the best player in the FIBA Basketball World Cup?
40. What is the name of the first player to dunk in a WNBA game?
41. What is the " FIBA window"?
42. What is the "clear path foul" rule in the NBA G League?
43. What is the "target score" rule in The Basketball Tournament (TBT)?
44. What is the "Elam Ending" in basketball?
45. What is the "coach's challenge" in the NBA?
46. What is the "advance step" rule in FIBA basketball?
47. What is the "EuroLeague Final Four"?
48. What is the "Basketball Africa League (BAL)"?
49. What is the "Jr. NBA"?
50. What is "3x3 basketball"?

Answers

1. Transition take foul: This rule, introduced in 2022, penalizes deliberate fouls committed to stop fast breaks. It aims to increase pace and excitement by discouraging these tactical fouls.
2. Loose ball foul vs. reach-in foul: A loose ball foul occurs when a player commits a foul while attempting to gain possession of a loose ball. A reach-in foul occurs when a defender reaches in and makes illegal contact with a ball-handler.
3. Ten-second violation: This violation occurs in the NBA when a team fails to advance the ball into the frontcourt within 10 seconds after a throw-in.
4. Lower defensive box: This area is a rectangle extending from the baseline to the free-throw line, used to determine defensive three-second violations. A defender cannot be in this area for more than three seconds without actively guarding an opponent.
5. Jump ball procedure: Historically, jump balls were used more frequently. Now, they primarily start the game and overtime periods. The possession arrow determines possession for other held ball situations.
6. Strong side: The strong side is the side of the court where the ball is located. Offensively, it's where most of

the action occurs. Defensively, players on the strong side need to be prepared for drives, screens, and shots.
7. Defensive three seconds: This rule prevents defenders from camping in the lane without actively guarding an opponent. It encourages more active defense and prevents clogging the lane.
8. Unsportsmanlike foul vs. technical foul: An unsportsmanlike foul is a personal foul that involves excessive or unnecessary contact, often away from the play. A technical foul is called for unsportsmanlike conduct, such as arguing or taunting.
9. Double dribble rule: A player cannot dribble with two hands simultaneously or dribble, stop, and then dribble again. This rule ensures continuous ball movement and prevents players from gaining an unfair advantage.
10. Penalty vs. bonus: The penalty situation is when a team has committed enough fouls to put the opposing team "in the bonus." The bonus means the opposing team gets free throws for each subsequent foul. The "penalty" is a specific term used in some leagues or levels of play.
11. Personal foul vs. common foul: A personal foul is any foul involving illegal contact with an opponent. A common foul is a type of personal foul that does not involve excessive contact or unsportsmanlike behavior.

12. Basket interference: This rule prohibits players from touching the ball or the basket while the ball is on the rim or within the cylinder above the rim. It also applies to touching the net while the ball is in the process of going through the basket.
13. Shot clock reset: The shot clock reset time varies depending on the league and the situation. For example, in the NBA, it resets to 14 seconds after an offensive rebound.
14. Quadruple-double: This rare feat occurs when a player records double-digits in four statistical categories in a single game. Nate Thurmond, Alvin Robertson, Hakeem Olajuwon, and David Robinson are the only NBA players to achieve this.
15. Team fouls: Each team is allowed a certain number of fouls per quarter (usually 5 in the NBA) before the opposing team enters the bonus. Team fouls reset each quarter.
16. Traveling violation during free throw: A player attempting a free throw cannot travel before releasing the ball. This includes moving their pivot foot or taking extra steps.
17. Illegal screen: A screen is illegal if the screener is moving or does not give the defender enough space to avoid contact. A legal screen involves the screener

being stationary and allowing the defender a reasonable opportunity to avoid contact.
18. Backcourt violation: This occurs when a player with the ball crosses the half-court line and then returns to the backcourt. Exceptions include deflected passes, steals, and loose balls.
19. Offensive basket interference: This occurs when an offensive player touches the ball or the basket while the ball is on the rim or within the cylinder above the rim, preventing a possible made basket.
20. Held ball violation: This term is not commonly used in basketball rules. A held ball situation is typically resolved with a jump ball or by using the possession arrow.
21. WNBA founded: 1996 (began play in 1997).
22. Magic and Bird's league: NBA (National Basketball Association).
23. "March Madness" coiner: Henry V. Porter, a former Illinois High School Association official.
24. First female NBA coach: Becky Hammon (assistant coach for the San Antonio Spurs).
25. Shortest NBA player: Muggsy Bogues (5'3").
26. Most wins in a season: Golden State Warriors (73 wins in the 2015-16 season).
27. 3 Finals MVPs with 3 teams: LeBron James (Miami Heat, Cleveland Cavaliers, Los Angeles Lakers).

28. All-Star Game MVP award: Kobe Bryant Trophy.
29. Sportsmanship award: Joe Dumars Trophy.
30. Teammate award: Twyman-Stokes Teammate of the Year Award.
31. First basketball video game: TV Basketball (released in 1974 for the Atari).
32. First Hall of Fame inductee: Dr. James Naismith (inducted in 1959).
33. Women's basketball Olympic debut: 1976 Montreal Olympics.
34. First Jordan shoe: Air Jordan 1 (released in 1985).
35. First back-to-back NBA champions: Minneapolis Lakers (1952 and 1953).
36. Youngest NBA draftee: Andrew Bynum (drafted at age 17 by the Los Angeles Lakers in 2005).
37. Oldest pro league: Liga Nacional de Básquetbol (Argentina), founded in 1893.
38. NBA, NCAA, and Olympic gold in the same year: Michael Jordan (1992).
39. FIBA World Cup MVP award: Most Valuable Player Award.
40. First WNBA dunk: Lisa Leslie (July 30, 2002).
41. FIBA window: Designated periods during the year when national teams can play official games, often interrupting club seasons.

42. G League clear path foul: Similar to the NBA rule, but the fouled player gets one free throw and their team retains possession.
43. Target score: In TBT, a game ends when a team reaches a target score (set 8 points above the leading team's score at the first dead ball under 4 minutes). This creates a more exciting finish.
44. Elam Ending: A format where the game clock is turned off at a certain point (e.g., under 4 minutes), and a target score is set. The first team to reach that score wins.
45. Coach's challenge: NBA coaches can challenge one call per game (if they have a timeout remaining). This allows for review of certain plays.
46. Advance step: In FIBA, a player can take one step in any direction with the ball before dribbling, allowing for more fluid movement.
47. EuroLeague Final Four: The final four teams in the EuroLeague playoffs compete in a single-elimination tournament to determine the champion.
48. Basketball Africa League (BAL): A professional basketball league in Africa, launched in 2020, featuring 12 club teams from different countries.
49. Jr. NBA: A youth basketball program that teaches fundamental skills and values to young players around the world.

50. 3x3 basketball: A variation of basketball played with three players on each team on a half-court. It's a fast-paced and exciting format that has gained popularity and is now an Olympic sport.

Chapter 4:
NOTEBOOK PAGES

1. What is the "transition take foul" rule, and why was it introduced?
2. Explain the difference between a "loose ball foul" and a "reach-in foul."
3. What is the "ten-second violation" in basketball, and when does it apply?
4. What is the "lower defensive box" in basketball, and how does it relate to defensive three-second violations?
5. Describe the "jump ball" procedure and how it has evolved over the years.

Notebook Prompt: Use this space to note any new basketball facts you learned from this section or ideas to share with fellow fans. You can also jot down any questions you have about these rules or how they are applied in different game situations.

....

....

....

....

....

....

....

....

....

....

6. What is the "strong side" in basketball, and how does it influence offensive and defensive strategies?
7. Explain the concept of "defensive three seconds" and its purpose in the NBA.
8. What is an "unsportsmanlike foul," and how is it different from a "technical foul"?
9. Describe the "double dribble" rule and the various ways players can violate it.
10. What is the "penalty" situation in basketball, and how does it differ from the "bonus" situation?

Notebook Prompt: Think about some games you've watched recently. Have you seen any of these rules come into play? How did they affect the game? Did the referees make any calls that you questioned or agreed with?

....

....

....

....

....

....

....

....

....

---

11. What is the difference between a "personal foul" and a "common foul"?
12. Explain the "basket interference" rule and how it applies to both offensive and defensive players.
13. What is the "shot clock reset" rule, and how can it vary depending on different leagues and situations?
14. What is a "quadruple-double" in basketball, and who are some players who have achieved it?

15. Explain the concept of "team fouls" in basketball and how they impact the game.

Notebook Prompt: If you were coaching a team, how would you teach your players about these rules and their importance in the game? What drills or strategies would you use to help them avoid violations and make smart decisions on the court?

....

....

....

....

....

....

....

....

---

16. What is a "traveling violation" during a free throw attempt?

17. What is an "illegal screen" in basketball, and what makes a screen legal?
18. Explain the "backcourt violation" in basketball and the exceptions to this rule.
19. What is the "offensive basket interference" rule?
20. What is a "held ball" violation in basketball, and how is it different from a "jump ball" situation?

Notebook Prompt: Imagine you're a referee. How would you make a call in a close situation involving one of these rules? What factors would you consider? How would you explain your decision to the players and coaches?

....

....

....

....

....

....

....

....

....

....

21. In what year was the WNBA founded?
22. What is the name of the basketball league in which Magic Johnson and Larry Bird played their iconic rivalry?
23. Who is credited with coining the term "March Madness"?
24. What is the name of the first woman to coach an NBA team?
25. Who was the shortest player to ever play in the NBA?

Notebook Prompt: Do you have a favorite WNBA player or team? What are some of the biggest differences you've noticed between the WNBA and the NBA?

....

....

....

....

....

....

....

....

....

26. Which NBA team holds the record for the most wins in a single season?
27. Who is the only player to win three consecutive NBA Finals MVP awards with three different teams?
28. What is the name of the award given to the most valuable player in the NBA All-Star Game?
29. What is the name of the award given to the player with the best sportsmanship in the NBA?
30. What is the name of the award given to the best teammate in the NBA?

Notebook Prompt: Which NBA awards do you think are the most prestigious? Why? If you could create a new NBA award, what would it be for?

....

....

....
....
....
....
....
....
....

31. What is the name of the first basketball video game?
32. Who was the first player to be inducted into the Naismith Memorial Basketball Hall of Fame?
33. In what year did women's basketball become an official Olympic sport?
34. What is the name of the first basketball shoe endorsed by Michael Jordan?
35. What is the name of the first basketball team to win back-to-back NBA championships?

Notebook Prompt: What are some of your favorite moments in basketball history? Which historical events or players do you find most inspiring?

....

....

....

....

....

....

....

....

....

36. Who is the youngest player to ever be drafted into the NBA?
37. What is the name of the oldest professional basketball league in the world still in operation?
38. Who is the only player to win an NBA championship, an NCAA championship, and an Olympic gold medal in the same year?
39. What is the name of the award given to the best player in the FIBA Basketball World Cup?
40. What is the name of the first player to dunk in a WNBA game?

Notebook Prompt: How has basketball changed over the years? What are some of the biggest differences between the game today and the game played decades ago?

....
....
....
....
....
....
....
....
....
....

41. What is the " FIBA window"?
42. What is the "clear path foul" rule in the NBA G League?
43. What is the "target score" rule in The Basketball Tournament (TBT)?

44. What is the "Elam Ending" in basketball?
45. What is the "coach's challenge" in the NBA?

Notebook Prompt: Do you think any of these newer rules or formats should be adopted by the NBA? Why or why not?

....
....
....
....
....
....
....
....
....

---

46. What is the "advance step" rule in FIBA basketball?
47. What is the "EuroLeague Final Four"?

48. What is the "Basketball Africa League (BAL)"?
49. What is the "Jr. NBA"?
50. What is "3x3 basketball"?

Notebook Prompt: What is the future of basketball? What new innovations or changes do you think we might see in the years to come?

....
....
....
....
....
....
....
....

Answers

1. Transition take foul: This rule, introduced in 2022, penalizes deliberate fouls committed to stop fast breaks. It aims to increase pace and excitement by discouraging these tactical fouls.
2. Loose ball foul vs. reach-in foul: A loose ball foul occurs when a player commits a foul while attempting to gain possession of a loose ball. A reach-in foul occurs when a defender reaches in and makes illegal contact with a ball-handler.
3. Ten-second violation: This violation occurs in the NBA when a team fails to advance the ball into the frontcourt within 10 seconds after a throw-in.
4. Lower defensive box: This area is a rectangle extending from the baseline to the free-throw line, used to determine defensive three-second violations. A defender cannot be in this area for more than three seconds without actively guarding an opponent.
5. Jump ball procedure: Historically, jump balls were used more frequently. Now, they primarily start the game and overtime periods. The possession arrow determines possession for other held ball situations.
6. Strong side: The strong side is the side of the court where the ball is located. Offensively, it's where most of

the action occurs. Defensively, players on the strong side need to be prepared for drives, screens, and shots.

7. Defensive three seconds: This rule prevents defenders from camping in the lane without actively guarding an opponent. It encourages more active defense and prevents clogging the lane.
8. Unsportsmanlike foul vs. technical foul: An unsportsmanlike foul is a personal foul that involves excessive or unnecessary contact, often away from the play. A technical foul is called for unsportsmanlike conduct, such as arguing or taunting.
9. Double dribble rule: A player cannot dribble with two hands simultaneously or dribble, stop, and then dribble again. This rule ensures continuous ball movement and prevents players from gaining an unfair advantage.
10. Penalty vs. bonus: The penalty situation is when a team has committed enough fouls to put the opposing team "in the bonus." The bonus means the opposing team gets free throws for each subsequent foul. The "penalty" is a specific term used in some leagues or levels of play.
11. Personal foul vs. common foul: A personal foul is any foul involving illegal contact with an opponent. A common foul is a type of personal foul that does not involve excessive contact or unsportsmanlike behavior.

12. Basket interference: This rule prohibits players from touching the ball or the basket while the ball is on the rim or within the cylinder above the rim. It also applies to touching the net while the ball is in the process of going through the basket.
13. Shot clock reset: The shot clock reset time varies depending on the league and the situation. For example, in the NBA, it resets to 14 seconds after an offensive rebound.
14. Quadruple-double: This rare feat occurs when a player records double-digits in four statistical categories in a single game. Nate Thurmond, Alvin Robertson, Hakeem Olajuwon, and David Robinson are the only NBA players to achieve this.
15. Team fouls: Each team is allowed a certain number of fouls per quarter (usually 5 in the NBA) before the opposing team enters the bonus. Team fouls reset each quarter.
16. Traveling violation during free throw: A player attempting a free throw cannot travel before releasing the ball. This includes moving their pivot foot or taking extra steps.
17. Illegal screen: A screen is illegal if the screener is moving or does not give the defender enough space to avoid contact. A legal screen involves the screener

being stationary and allowing the defender a reasonable opportunity to avoid contact.
18. Backcourt violation: This occurs when a player with the ball crosses the half-court line and then returns to the backcourt. Exceptions include deflected passes, steals, and loose balls.
19. Offensive basket interference: This occurs when an offensive player touches the ball or the basket while the ball is on the rim or within the cylinder above the rim, preventing a possible made basket.
20. Held ball violation: This term is not commonly used in basketball rules. A held ball situation is typically resolved with a jump ball or by using the possession arrow.
21. WNBA founded: 1996 (began play in 1997).
22. Magic and Bird's league: NBA (National Basketball Association).
23. "March Madness" coiner: Henry V. Porter, a former Illinois High School Association official.
24. First female NBA coach: Becky Hammon (assistant coach for the San Antonio Spurs).
25. Shortest NBA player: Muggsy Bogues (5'3").
26. Most wins in a season: Golden State Warriors (73 wins in the 2015-16 season).
27. 3 Finals MVPs with 3 teams: LeBron James (Miami Heat, Cleveland Cavaliers, Los Angeles Lakers).

28. All-Star Game MVP award: Kobe Bryant Trophy.
29. Sportsmanship award: Joe Dumars Trophy.
30. Teammate award: Twyman-Stokes Teammate of the Year Award.
31. First basketball video game: TV Basketball (released in 1974 for the Atari).
32. First Hall of Fame inductee: Dr. James Naismith (inducted in 1959).
33. Women's basketball Olympic debut: 1976 Montreal Olympics.
34. First Jordan shoe: Air Jordan 1 (released in 1985).
35. First back-to-back NBA champions: Minneapolis Lakers (1952 and 1953).
36. Youngest NBA draftee: Andrew Bynum (drafted at age 17 by the Los Angeles Lakers in 2005).
37. Oldest pro league: Liga Nacional de Básquetbol (Argentina), founded in 1893.
38. NBA, NCAA, and Olympic gold in the same year: Michael Jordan (1992).
39. FIBA World Cup MVP award: Most Valuable Player Award.
40. First WNBA dunk: Lisa Leslie (July 30, 2002).
41. FIBA window: Designated periods during the year when national teams can play official games, often interrupting club seasons.

42. G League clear path foul: Similar to the NBA rule, but the fouled player gets one free throw and their team retains possession.
43. Target score: In TBT, a game ends when a team reaches a target score (set 8 points above the leading team's score at the first dead ball under 4 minutes). This creates a more exciting finish.
44. Elam Ending: A format where the game clock is turned off at a certain point (e.g., under 4 minutes), and a target score is set. The first team to reach that score wins.
45. Coach's challenge: NBA coaches can challenge one call per game (if they have a timeout remaining). This allows for review of certain plays.
46. Advance step: In FIBA, a player can take one step in any direction with the ball before dribbling, allowing for more fluid movement.
47. EuroLeague Final Four: The final four teams in the EuroLeague playoffs compete in a single-elimination tournament to determine the champion.
48. Basketball Africa League (BAL): A professional basketball league in Africa, launched in 2020, featuring 12 club teams from different countries.
49. Jr. NBA: A youth basketball program that teaches fundamental skills and values to young players around the world.

50. 3x3 basketball: A variation of basketball played with three players on each team on a half-court. It's a fast-paced and exciting format that has gained popularity and is now an Olympic sport.

The contents of this book may not be copied, reproduced or transmitted without the express written permission of the author or publisher. Under no circumstances will the publisher or author be responsible or liable for any damages, compensation or monetary loss arising from the information contained in this book, whether directly or indirectly. .

Disclaimer Notice:

Although the author and publisher have made every effort to ensure the accuracy and completeness of the content, they do not, however, make any representations or warranties as to the accuracy, completeness, or reliability of the content. , suitability or availability of the information, products, services or related graphics contained in the book for any purpose. Readers are solely responsible for their use of the information contained in this book

Every effort has been made to make this book possible. If any omission or error has occurred unintentionally, the author and publisher will be happy to acknowledge it in upcoming versions.

Copyright © 2024

All rights reserved.

Printed in Great Britain
by Amazon